AF609345

Designing for Local Communities

Designing for Local Communities

A guide to freelancing and empowering groups in your neighborhood

Meaghan Barry

BLOOMSBURY VISUAL ARTS
LONDON • NEW YORK • OXFORD • NEW DELHI • SYDNEY

BLOOMSBURY VISUAL ARTS
Bloomsbury Publishing Plc, 50 Bedford Square, London, WC1B 3DP, UK
Bloomsbury Publishing Inc, 1385 Broadway, New York, NY 10018, USA
Bloomsbury Publishing Ireland, 29 Earlsfort Terrace, Dublin 2, D02 AY28, Ireland

BLOOMSBURY, BLOOMSBURY VISUAL ARTS and the Diana logo are trademarks of Bloomsbury Publishing Plc

First published in Great Britain 2025

Copyright © Meaghan Barry, 2025

Meaghan Barry has asserted her right under the Copyright, Designs and Patents Act, 1988, to be identified as author of this work.

For legal purposes the Acknowledgments on p. xiv constitute an extension of this copyright page.

Cover design: Meaghan Barry
Cover image © Meaghan Barry

All rights reserved. No part of this publication may be: i) reproduced or transmitted in any form, electronic or mechanical, including photocopying, recording or by means of any information storage or retrieval system without prior permission in writing from the publishers; or ii) used or reproduced in any way for the training, development or operation of artificial intelligence (AI) technologies, including generative AI technologies. The rights holders expressly reserve this publication from the text and data mining exception as per Article 4(3) of the Digital Single Market Directive (EU) 2019/790.

Bloomsbury Publishing Plc does not have any control over, or responsibility for, any third-party websites referred to or in this book. All internet addresses given in this book were correct at the time of going to press. The author and publisher regret any inconvenience caused if addresses have changed or sites have ceased to exist, but can accept no responsibility for any such changes.

A catalogue record for this book is available from the British Library.

A catalogue record for this book is available from the Library of Congress.

ISBN: HB: 978-1-3504-0095-5
PB: 978-1-3504-0096-2
ePDF: 978-1-3504-0097-9
eBook: 978-1-3504-0098-6

Typeset by Integra Software Services Pvt. Ltd.
Printed and Bound in Great Britain by Bell & Bain Ltd, Glasgow

For product safety related questions contact productsafety@bloomsbury.com.

To find out more about our authors and books visit www.bloomsbury.com and sign up for our newsletters.

Contents

Preface

I've been teaching graphic design at a university in the suburbs of Detroit, Michigan for over a decade, and every year my students ask if they need to move to a bigger city, such as New York City, London, or Los Angeles to really "make it" in the industry. Like them, I thought I had to move to a well-known urban area and work for global corporations such as Apple, Google, or Nike to be deemed successful. I grew up in a rural farm town in Massachusetts, and I fled to Brooklyn, New York to study Communications Design at Pratt Institute in the mid-2000s because of this idea.

The sentiment was reiterated by my city friends in 2010, when I decided to move to Bloomfield Hills, Michigan for graduate studies in 2D Design at Cranbrook Academy of Art. They'd ask me, "Why would you *ever* want to leave New York City to go to *Michigan*?" with a grimace to emphasize their feelings about my upcoming place of residence. My reply was that I'd return, but I never did and have no immediate plans to do so.

My aim with this book is to dispel the myth that you must live in a "designer city" or work for name brand clients to be considered a "real" designer. Staying in Michigan, I've built an award-winning design studio based in Detroit, by primarily working with small businesses in my community. If I had stayed in New York City, I'm not sure if I would or could have done this, especially at such a young age; Lilian Crum and I launched Unsold Studio in 2013, when I was twenty-five years old. Detroit, a city that filed bankruptcy that same year,[1] presented its own challenges for starting a business, but its smaller size, lower cost of living, and non-saturation of design studios offered a clear opening in the market for us. My intention is not to dismiss the desire to work for big clients in a big city, but rather I want to offer another possibility for a fulfilling career: designing for your local community, wherever that is.

Designers help preserve and create character in communities. We build visual culture that gives our towns, cities, and regions identifiable qualities and charm. If we do not want to lose our main streets filled with mom-and-pop shops and cities with unique neighborhoods, we have to prioritize making for local businesses and organizations. Otherwise, every place will begin to look the same, filled with corporate box stores and chain restaurants. Don't get me wrong, I love the familiarity those types of places provide us, but I do not love the monoculture they create. With my design skills, I'd prefer to empower the folks from my neighborhood, improve our local visual culture, and invest in the place I call home.

Tending to your neighborhood in this way may seem charitable or altruistic, but it can also be a selfish act (in a good way). When I ask my students who their dream clients are, they never say the laundromat or pharmacy down the street with the modest budget. However, when I interviewed small independent design studios from across the globe, featured throughout this book, these types of projects are

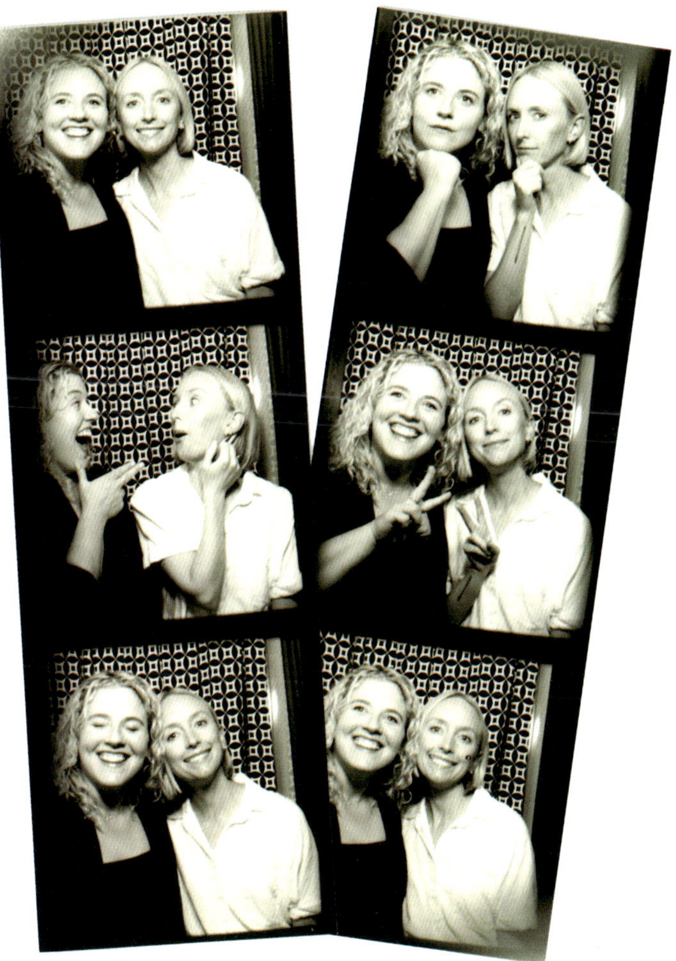

Figure 0.1 Unsold Studio design partners, Meaghan Barry (author; left) and Lilian Crum (right). Image courtesy of Unsold Studio.

the foundation to their successes. While our cultures vary, this experience echoed across our stories. *Every* person I spoke with landed their first big client from within their community. It was not from winning awards, sending out press releases, blog features, a large social media audience, or running advertisements. Instead, it was their local client, a friend, a family member, or a neighbor who recommended them and helped grow their design practice.

For a long time, I felt embarrassed my design studio had not landed a huge client with a gigantic budget, such as Netflix or Target. Sometimes, I still do. However, after chatting with these designers from around the globe, I'm reminded that the work I've done close to home is important. I've built a career, but also developed

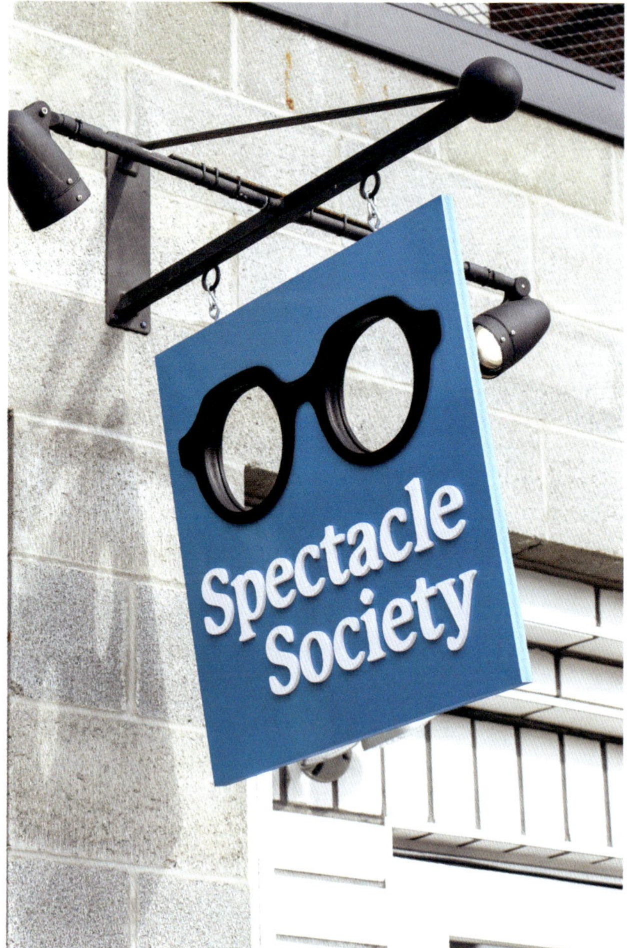

Figure 0.2 Store signage for Unsold Studio's branding client, Spectacle Society, an optician located in the Corktown neighborhood of Detroit, Michigan. Image courtesy of Unsold Studio / Photograph by J. Lindsey Photography.

a sense of pride for where I live. We must celebrate small-scale work, build confidence in "quieter" design careers, and see value in championing our communities with our design talent.

You might be thinking, "This all sounds great, but how do you actually start taking on this kind of work?" My answer is freelancing, but this might be a scary proposition for you, and you're not alone.

At the university where I teach, I authored a course for my undergraduate students titled *Professional Practices for Graphic Design*. In the first half of the course, students learn about "Working for Others" with topics such as portfolio creation, cover letter writing, interview skills, and navigating their first junior design job. In

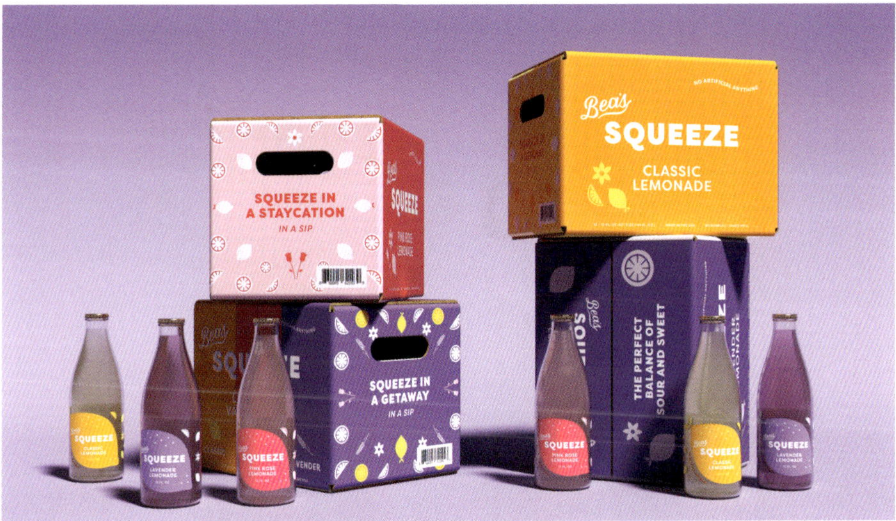

Figure 0.3 Unsold Studio rebranded Bea's Squeeze, a Detroit-based beverage company, to help bring their lemonade to a national market. 3D rendering by Alessandro Pagura. Image courtesy of Unsold Studio / 3D rendering by Alessandro Pagura.

developing this section of the curriculum, I found ample resources targeted for emerging designers, and my students seemed more comfortable with these topics.

However, the second half of the course, "Working for Self," where students learn freelancing skills such as proposal development, pricing, and project management skills, they were more hesitant. The available resources on these topics catered to a more advanced audience; many publications assume the reader has some "real-world" design experience with an established network to begin their independent practice. Their advice is intended for a reader who plans to freelance full time, hire employees, and/or acquire large client accounts. When I presented these types of publications in the course, my students were intimidated by their business and legal language and the large-scale scopes of work the information was intended to cover. Many of my students initially expressed that they "could never take on freelancing work" if this is what it entailed. Interestingly, by the end of the semester once I had simplified and curated the information to their needs, such as taking on a project for a friend or small business, their confidence increased. My aim is to offer you the same assurance by tailoring this publication for the true beginner freelancer.

According to the US Bureau of Labor Statistics in 2020,[2] 19 percent of graphic designers were self-employed, yet a 2019 survey commissioned by Upwork and the Freelancers Union[3] found "75% of workers in the greater Arts & Design industry regularly take on freelance work." And for transparency, I fit into this 75 percent because I'm not fully self-employed. While I co-own a design studio and do consistent client work, I continue to hold a full-time position as an Associate Professor of Graphic Design. At my university job, I receive a steady paycheck, health care, retirement, and other benefits that provide me stability. My freelance work has increased

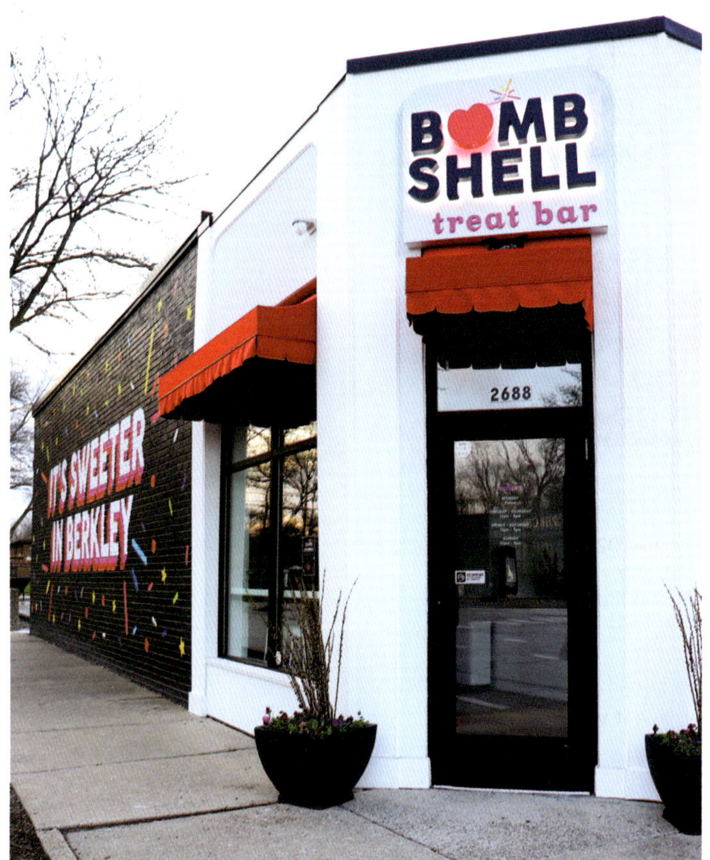

Figure 0.4 Unsold Studio designed the brand identity for Bombshell Treat Bar, which opened its first brick-and-mortar location in Berkley, Michigan in April 2024. The exterior mural design implemented the brand elements to create a sense of place and pride for the small suburban city the store is located in. Mural installed by sign painter Jordan Zielke.

my income, connected me with design and business networks, and served as the foundation of my academic research. Even with all these positives, I've never gone fully independent, and you do not need to either (unless you really want to).

Like my students, I had one optional elective course in my undergraduate education titled *Freelancing & Business*. Primarily, my design education prepared and encouraged me to enter the workforce in a traditional nine-to-five office experience as a junior designer. Despite having some access to design business education at university, it was not enough. In 2013, Lilian—my Cranbrook Academy of Art 2D design studio mate—and I discussed how we were both interested in doing freelance design work post-graduation, but agreed it felt daunting to start alone. In that moment, we decided without hesitation to partner up. We used a random word generator to come up with "Unsold Studio," designed a logo, took some headshots

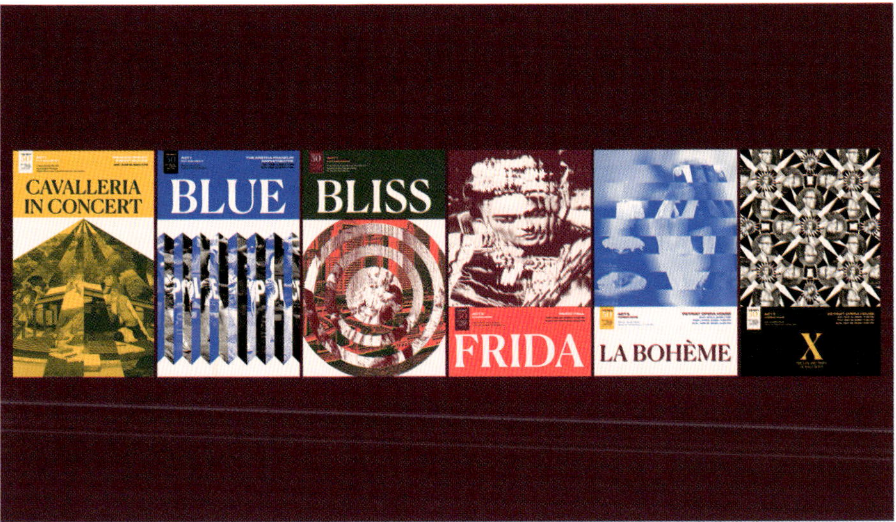

Figure 0.5 For the 2021–2 Michigan Opera Theatre season, Unsold Studio developed promotional imagery such as show posters, to make opera inclusive and cool in the city of Detroit. Image courtesy of Unsold Studio.

(which looked like bad band photographs), and launched a website on it with no portfolio (we felt like it was disingenuous to not have true collaborative work on the site).

We quickly discovered that while we were good designers, we were not good businesspeople. Luckily, a design advocacy group, Design Core Detroit (then the Detroit Creative Corridor Center), offered a program called the "Creative Ventures Residency Program," which functioned like a six-month business bootcamp. In 2014, we were one of four businesses selected to participate. We were partnered with a lawyer, an accountant, and other experts to learn business skills catered to creatives. Lilian and I credit this program with helping us "level up," but few designers have access to these types of programs or resources in their communities. My aim is to increase access to design business education by creating a more equitable resource—this cost-effective publication that you can access at any time—rather than one that is cost-prohibitive, juried, location- and/or time-specific.

With most designers freelancing at some point in their careers, we need more resources that are tailored to sporadic independent work. This book is intended for designers who will take on a freelance project from time-to-time or who are gradually establishing an independent practice, rather than a designer who is ready to be fully self-employed. This is your how-to manual for your first foray into freelancing, to help you avoid some of the mistakes I learned from along the way. You'll still have your own "failures" and there will be more to learn beyond these pages, but it will give you the basics to begin taking on local small businesses, nonprofits, and individuals as clients. Freelancing in your neighborhood is an act that will benefit your community, as well as your own design career. No matter where you live, I'm confident there is design work to be had.

How to use this book

I've designed this publication to function as a *Choose Your Own Adventure*-type book. You should start in the section you need the most. Use Figure 0.6 as a visual guide to determine where to begin. For example, if you have a potential client looking to work together, you'll begin in Chapter 2, "If someone is interested in working with you," whereas if you're looking for your first client, you'll flip to Chapter 1, "If you need to find a freelance project." Throughout the book, there will be prompts and directions to lead you to the information you need based on your specific situation. Every time you pick up this publication, your journey with it may be a bit different. Of course, you can also read it cover to cover, but its design is meant to focus you on what you need to know in the moment and avoid information overload.

Embedded throughout, in featured interviews, I present new design heroes, whose work embodies the ethos of this book. They were selected because of their boutique size (individual designers, partnerships, or small studios of less than ten employees) and their location in places that do not rank first when you google "best design cities in the world." Their stories are meant to feel familiar; I want you to see yourself in them. I want their career journeys, their clients, and their portfolios to feel attainable, which was rarely the experience I had learning about designers in history books and university classrooms. I want these types of people, those who are empowering their communities with design, to inspire the next generation of designers and freelancers.

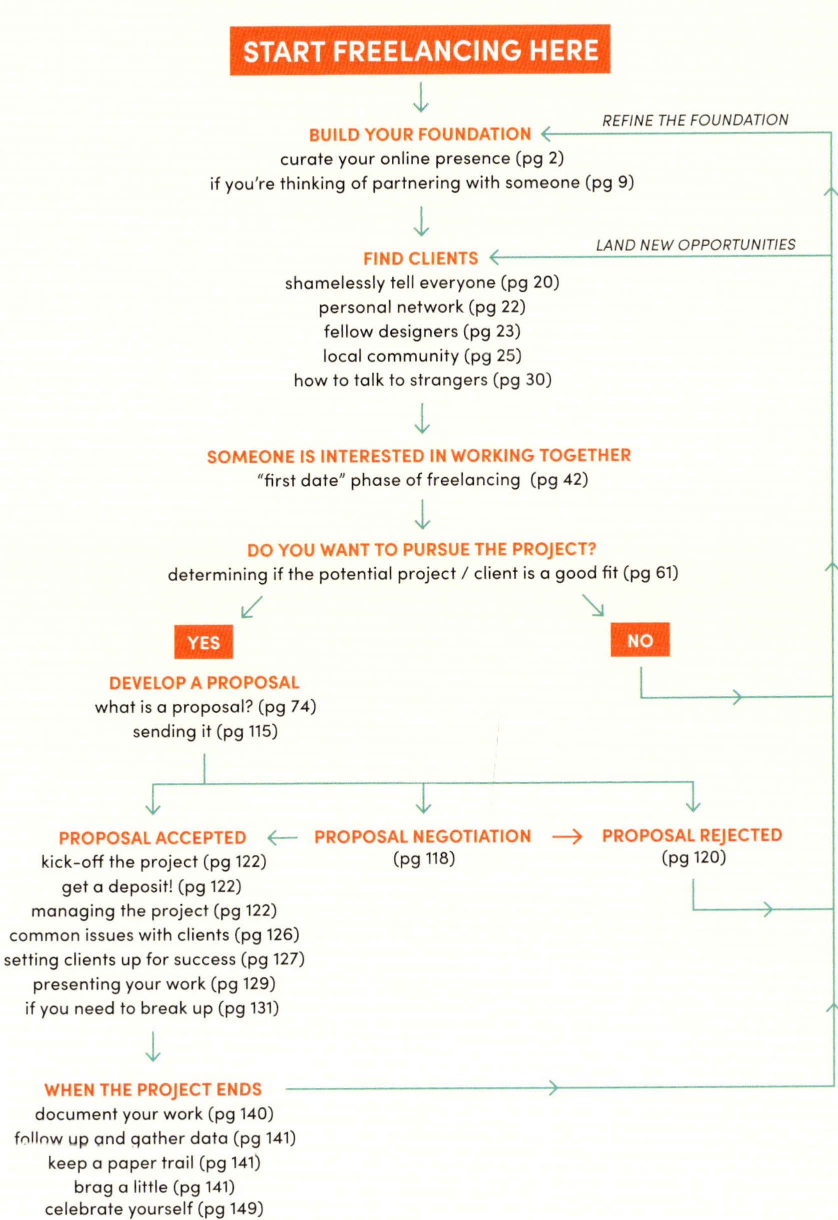

Figure 0.6 Infographic for navigating the publication.

Acknowledgments

This book is an amalgamation of many different periods and people in my professional and personal lives, and my gratitude extends throughout:

To Mom, for your consistent belief and investment in my capabilities. To Dad, for your inspiring work ethic and career bravery. To the rest of my family and friends, for your unwavering love and support.

To all my teachers and mentors: Cheryl Adams who introduced me to graphic design and set me on this creative path; at Pratt Institute, particularly Kathleen Creighton and Jon Weiman who co-taught our freelancing fundamentals course; at Cranbrook Academy of Art, Elliott Earls who made critical writing essential; and later Meredith Kerekes, via Design Core Detroit, who taught me many of the business essentials covered in this publication.

To all my colleagues at Oakland University, thank you for the camaraderie and for making me a better educator and creative. To my students, this book would not exist without you.

To Lilian Crum for being my business and creative partner for over a decade at Unsold Studio, and friend for even longer.

To all the clients who have hired and trusted Unsold Studio, and who were patient with me as I learned—and continue to learn—along the way.

To all the interviewees and contributors, thank you for believing in this project and agreeing to be a part of it. Collecting your stories was the highlight of this process, and I'm so excited to share them with readers.

To Dr. Marcella Sutcliffe's Chapelgarth Writing Retreat and Michigan State University's Community-Engaged Scholarship Writing Retreat for giving space and time for me to write. To all my writer friends, such as Christin Lee, who provided feedback and encouragement during the process.

To the Design Incubation network, who planted a book writing seed many years ago, and who introduced me to Louise Baird-Smith and the Bloomsbury team through their programming. Louise and Joseph Skingsley, thank you for your advocacy and work on this project.

And finally, to Fernando, my forever teammate.

Designing for Local Communities

1

If you need to find a freelance project

One of the common questions my students ask is, "How do I find clients?" Many of them express that they lack connections and find networking intimidating. If you're like them, this is where you want to begin.

Build your foundation

In this section, you'll prepare the freelancing fundamentals, such as an online presence, *before* engaging with potential clients. This way, when you do approach them, you will feel confident and put your best self forward. Designer Gareth Strange from John & Jane (interview, page 13) agrees with this approach, saying: "We put a lot into our website and made sure our brand was cohesive across every client touch point before we started promoting our services."

Once that's complete, *then* we'll address where to find clients. You'll identify multiple channels to acquire design projects and learn that you're more well connected than you think. And if you're a little shy, I also have some tips for putting yourself out there.

Curate your online presence

Your online presence is one of the first interactions potential clients will have with you and your work, so you need to make a good impression. To make a great one, I've outlined key elements you need online to effectively attract and land client work.

The basics

If you're just starting out, you need two essential things:

1. ***A place online where someone can view samples of your design work.***

   When you begin pitching your design services to folks, I guarantee as part of the conversation, they will ask to see an example of your work. You have to be ready to share your portfolio in some form, whether that's a website or a social media profile. This does not have to be over-designed or fancy—it simply needs to show off your best work quickly and easily for the viewer.

   For portfolio websites, template builders such as Adobe Portfolio, Squarespace, and Wix are *totally* acceptable to use. These types of sites do have a cost associated with them, so check their pricing before committing to a platform. (*Pro tip: if you have a .edu or student email address, you can get usually get a discount.*) Free community-based sites such as Behance and Dribble are a good choice if budget is a concern. Unless you are looking to be a web or app developer, your portfolio can be straightforward and use the default features these templates offer. It's hard enough to keep your site updated (refreshing Unsold Studio's site is the bane of my existence), so avoid roadblocks such as custom coding, especially if that's not your thing.

   In the past few years, I've found more people visit Unsold Studio's Instagram profile (@unsoldstudio) before they head to our dedicated website. This trend is something I've spoken with my design friends about; how our social media feeds have become our primary portfolios because they are so easy to "post-and-go." If you decide to share your work this way, consider making the profile public; it removes the viewing barrier of a friend request. You'll also want to curate your feed a bit more closely, deciding what you feel comfortable being seen as part of your professional freelancing persona.

   I advise my students when curating projects for their portfolios that I'd rather see quality over quantity. For instance, I'd prefer to see only three very strong projects, rather than three very strong projects mixed among six less-than-stellar projects. This means don't let a "lack" of examples hold you back; start with the few things that best represent you and add more over time.

   If you need more work to populate your portfolio, create your own projects or include process or "failed" work. Designer Josh Carnley from Matey (interview, page 50) said he kept his freelance portfolio up to date while working at his full-time design job by making mock projects for himself, for instance, designing a brand for a company that made pennant banners. Search project brief generators online if you need a jumping-off point. I also recommend offering your services at low- or no-cost to your family, friends, small businesses, or nonprofits that need design to give you a real client experience to feature in your portfolio when you're starting out (if you want to go down this route, see "Personal network" and "Local community," in this chapter). Your local network is one of your best assets, so that's why I advocate for leveraging it to fill in portfolio gaps, rather than doing speculative work—also known as "spec work"—where the designer provides creative work to a client prior to receiving compensation. A design competition is a form of "spec work" because only the winning designer might receive a cash prize. It's also likely the fine print of the competition rules states that the client owns all the submitted creative work, even those they do not select as winners, which means they receive a lot of design work for free. If you're going to give away anything, give it to folks and causes you care about rather than a stranger on the internet.

There is a ton of available resources related to portfolio development, such as *Creating a Successful Graphic Design Portfolio* by Irina Lee, if you're looking for more in-depth information about the topic.

2. ***A way for people to communicate with you.***

   An email account is the primary communication tool you'll need. Email is my first choice because it keeps a written, time-stamped record of the communication between you and your client. It allows you to easily refer back to information the client provides you, such as project details and feedback. If disagreements arise (fingers crossed they will not), there is a paper trail to help resolve issues.

   Sharing your telephone number or other contact points is up to you, and what you feel comfortable with. For instance, I do not advertise my personal phone number and only give it to clients as needed. I prefer to set this boundary as a way to keep me focused during the workday. If a client texts or calls me, I feel like I have to reply or answer straight away, which disrupts my workflow. With email, I feel less pressure to respond instantly, and this gives me a chance to collect my thoughts before getting back to them.

   By having email as my main contact point for clients, it's much easier to manage communication—I do not have to search my direct messages, look at phone call logs, and text message threads to remember the deadline the client asked me for. I recommend streamlining your communication through one primary channel, such as email, to keep you organized.

   Ultimately, as long as folks know how to best get hold of you, and that you respond to them, is what matters. And to emphasize, responding is super important. No one likes to be "left on read" or "ghosted." Get back to people who've contacted you within a reasonable time frame: in the United States, where I'm based, 24–48 hours of normal business hours, 9:00 a.m. to 5:00 p.m., Monday through Friday. We'll talk more about setting communication boundaries in "That scary legal language" (in Chapter 3) and "Managing the project" (in Chapter 4). Flip there if you'd like to learn more about its impact on your freelancing work now.

If you're just beginning to take on design projects, these two things will get you by: an online portfolio and an email address. If you have these essentials ready to go, you can skip ahead in this chapter to "Find clients," if you feel ready. However, I'd recommend "upgrading" with the list of items below, especially as you seek out and take on more freelancing work. These recommendations are meant to enhance how potential clients perceive you as a hirable designer. In my experience, folks are more inclined to commission you—and pay higher rates—if you come across as professional and intentional. By tailoring your public-facing elements—such as your portfolio, email address, and social media handles—to your target audience of potential clients, you'll definitely improve your freelancing game.

The upgrades

Tailor your portfolio site to be more freelancing-specific

In design school, you're taught how to put together a portfolio. At that point, the goal is usually to impress more senior designers in hopes they hire you. However, when you're building a design business, the audience for your portfolio shifts to potential clients who are often *not* designers. My clients are coffee roasters, nonprofit leaders, spa owners, and ice cream makers who are experts at their craft, *not* design. When looking at your portfolio, they do not need the design nerd things that will impress a senior art director looking to add you to their team. Instead, potential clients have a different set of questions that your portfolio needs to answer.

Examples of questions a potential client might have:

- ***Does the designer's work fit my aesthetic?*** Your style is either going to resonate with them or it isn't. While you should always be honing your design skills, this is a subjective decision by the potential client that you have less control over.
- ***What is their design area of expertise?*** Your portfolio demonstrates what you're capable of producing for clients. What you feature in your portfolio is the type of work you will attract. If all you show in your portfolio is logo design, that is all you will get hired to do, whereas if you share logo design, web design, and app design, you're communicating that you offer a wider range of design services. However, more is not always better. If the potential client wants a logo, they'll likely hire the logo expert. The key is to make sure your portfolio showcases the type of work *you* want to take on.
- ***Will this designer solve my problem(s)?*** As mentioned, many potential clients are not designers themselves, so they might not be able to articulate exactly what they need from you using design terminology. Showing a list of your services is great, but if the person does not know the difference between terms such as "brand strategy" and "brand identity," that does not help them much. However, potential clients do know they are looking to hire

you to increase revenue for their company, launch a new product, or engage a new target audience. This is why it is important to reframe your projects to demonstrate your problem-solving skills, especially through your written project descriptions.

Example: *I designed a website for a bakery using Adobe XD.* **vs** *The bakery website was designed to increase online sales by simplifying the ordering process for the customer.*

It's also important to write in simple terms, avoiding industry jargon. Imagine you're talking about your business to a non-designer in your life. For me, this is my mom. Throughout my career, I've asked her to review things such as project descriptions: if they make sense to her, they pass the test.

Example: *I kerned the wordmark.* **vs** *I enhanced the legibility of the logo by increasing the space between individual letters.*

- ***What would it be like to work with this designer?*** Some of your prospective clients may never have hired a designer before, which can be intimidating! They're getting ready to spend their hard-earned money on something they're unfamiliar with. They might not understand the process, the costs, or what questions to ask. Your site should make these newbies comfortable. A few ideas on how to do this are:
    - Make sure your portfolio communicates "investment-worthy." This sounds complicated, but it isn't. You simply need to demonstrate that you're professional, pay attention to details, and "practice what you preach" with good design. If your site is disorganized, requires too many mouse clicks, or is riddled with spelling errors, it will not instill confidence that you're the designer I trust with my project.
    - Feature a "case study"—a detailed description of a portfolio project that shows the different phases of your design process and demonstrates your thinking and problem-solving. This differs from a standard portfolio entry where the viewer only sees the finished and polished results, accompanied by a short description of the work. If you write a case study, make sure you include information about the client's role throughout the process as well—this will help a prospective client see how they might work with you more clearly.
    - Educate the potential client in a friendly way. For instance, perhaps there is a quick step-by-step overview of your design process so they can learn what to expect if they work with you.
    - Show yourself off! People hire people they feel a connection with. If you're hiding behind your work, you're missing an opportunity to connect with someone. Write a quick bio and snap a quick headshot. Write the site's language so it sounds like your voice.
    - If you have current or past clients that loved your work, ask for testimonials from them that you can publish on your site. Hearing how you've helped others can be insightful for a prospective client.

- *I'm interested in working with the designer—what are the next steps?* Make it easy to contact you! You could include a form to fill out that guides them in communicating their project details, such as goals, timeline, and budget, which will ultimately help you.

Select an official freelancing business name

When you begin freelancing, you'll probably just be known as yourself—this totally works. However, at some point, you might decide that you want to assign an official name to your freelancing work. This might make you feel more professional and/or help you separate your personal identity from your work identity.

If you're considering names, you must conduct research to make sure that your freelancing business name will be easy to remember, find online, and not be confused with others. Questions to ask yourself during the selection process are:

- Will the name consistently challenge your target audience—is it hard to say or spell?
- Is a website domain name available and affordable?
- Are social media handles available?
- Are there any other businesses with the same or similar names, especially in the design industry?

Naming yourself is not an easy task, but I've outlined two options to help you:

OPTION ONE: Use your own name You do not have to over think it—it can be this simple! However, if you have a common name, you might consider adding another word such as "design" or "studio" to help differentiate yourself. Google your own name to see who you're "competing" with to determine if using your name is a good idea. For instance, there is another Meaghan Barry, a Toronto-based information designer and artist, I've been confused with. Due to this, I might choose Option Two.

OPTION TWO: Use an alternative name You can also use something besides your name, such as Alessandra Corbett who operates under the Homegrown Studio (interview, page 32) or my illustrator friend Courtney Jentzen known as Swiss Cottage Designs. My business partner Lilian and I used a random word generator to select Unsold Studio because we were having a hard time selecting a name. "Unsold" was one of the first words to appear, and when it did, we both had a positive reaction. It felt a little diamond-in-the-rough (that is why our logo is shaped that way), a little underdog, and not overly corporate, which felt like us. We also loved that when Unsold Studio was shortened, it spelled "us," which felt collaborative and spoke to our partnership. From a business perspective, the moniker "Unsold" was also good because it's an uncommon word. This meant things such as domain names and social media handles were available. It's become a great conversation starter when we introduce ourselves because people always ask the story behind the unique name.

Whatever you choose, it's important that you feel comfortable saying it and typing it—you'll be doing both of those things a lot. If it doesn't feel good to you, it definitely will not for others. Practice saying your top choice out loud and run it by a trusted (and honest) friend before committing.

If you've chosen an official business name, more upgrades include:

- Purchasing the website domain name and linking it to your portfolio site.
- Creating business-specific social media accounts.
- Getting a custom email address that's just for business.

  A new inbox that is reserved only for business communication will keep you organized. You will not be sorting through personal emails and spam when working. When we first started out, we acquired a free Gmail account: unsoldstudio@gmail.com. The default "gmail.com" at the end looked a bit amateur, but our clients knew where to get hold of us and we'd answer.

  Eventually when we had more client projects and income, we upgraded to a Google Workspace account that allowed us to create a custom email address: hello@unsoldstudio.com. Shifting to the @unsoldstudio.com email ending communicates a more professional setup to prospective clients. While this does have a cost attached, the Google Workspace account comes with Gmail, but also Google tools such as Calendar, Drive, and Sheets that makes life with our clients easier. Google Workspace can be purchased directly, or it is available for seamless integration in most website builders such as Squarespace and Wix for an additional monthly fee. There are other providers and tools you can use to create a custom email address. Do some research and decide what works best for you.

- Registering the business name with the appropriate government organization (if applicable).

  The primary reason you register your business name is for legal and tax purposes. Each federal, state, and local government entity will have its own processes and requirements for its small businesses. As a reminder, I'm a designer and a professor, not a legal expert, so you will need to do a bit of your own research to determine what steps you need to take for your design business to be in a good legal standing depending on where you live.

  If you're not sure where to find this type of information, I recommend reaching out to other local small business owners. They will serve as great mentors because they've already navigated these legal processes. Most likely, there are also government organizations, programs, and community groups that can help you navigate setting up your small business. For example, where I'm located, we have the US Small Business Administration. Their website is full of information, such as how to determine if you need to register your business name. According to their site,[1] in the United States:

  - If you're a one-person owned business, you likely do not have to register your business name if you're operating under your legal name. This is because the government will see you and your business as one and the same. For filing taxes, you will use your social security number as your Tax ID.

- If you're operating under something other than your legal name, you most likely will need to file a *"DBA,"* which stands for *"Doing Business As."* This lets the government know that your business name and your legal identity are connected. For filing taxes, you will still use your social security number as your Tax ID.
- There are other business structures you can register for in the United States, such as an *"LLC"—a limited liability company—which protects you from personal liability if your business faces bankruptcy or lawsuits,*[2] which is a common choice for small-scale design studios. There are more legal and financial hoops to jump through for these types of entities (your taxes definitely get more complicated), however, the perk is that they protect your personal assets. For example, if a client sues you, your house, car, motorcycle, boat, and so on, are not at risk—only the assets the LLC owns will be. However, with the first two options, your personal and business assets are together, so all your assets would be at risk. For filing taxes as an LLC, you will need to acquire an *"EIN"—an Employer Identification Number—which functions as your business' Tax ID.*

See "Local community," in Chapter 2, to identify established business networks that can help you navigate your government's rules and regulations. If you're regularly acquiring freelance work, I highly recommend connecting with professionals such as accountants and lawyers to give you personalized legal and financial advice. While the upfront cost might feel like a lot, over time, your investment in their services will save you money, time, and lots of headaches.

If you're thinking of partnering with someone

I hit the lottery finding a design business partner, and a friend, in Lilian: we've been running Unsold Studio for over ten years and somehow, we still like to hang out together on the weekends. Having her there to bounce ideas off of, pick up my slack when I'm struggling, and vent to has kept me sane while freelancing. We often say to one another on particularly stressful days, "I can't imagine trying to do this by myself." While you absolutely can take on client work solo, if you're thinking about partnering up with someone, consider:

Are you willing to risk your current relationship?

Unfortunately, this is a reality you have to contend with when you go into business with someone that you're close to. While starting a studio with a friend is much more fun, the stresses of running it over time will wear on you and your relationship. Inevitably, there will be moments where you'll disagree with one another. That's when it can be hard to separate the business from the personal. While it can be easy to say, "That will never happen to us," you need to be realistic about what could happen, and if that's worth it to you. Some good questions to ask yourself are:

- Have you collaborated on a project together before? If yes, how did it go? If no, could you do a "test run" before making the partnership official?
- Does your potential partner have traits that already get on your nerves—for instance, are they always running late? Will these characteristics be amplified or problematic in a business scenario?
- Are you willing to challenge your friend over a business decision? Will it bother you if they challenge you?
- Will you be able to set boundaries between your freelancing partnership and your current relationship? Are you capable of leaving work at work?

Does your potential partner complement you?

The best partner will be someone who is not exactly like you; someone who has different interests and expertise, especially in the areas where you might be weaker. For instance, I love to focus on the big ideas in a project, but following through on the vital detail work is not my favorite. Luckily, Lilian is detail-oriented and thrives where I do not. Similarly, while Lilian is more reserved, I'm more outgoing. This yin and yang quality is a common theme in successful partnerships.

When I interviewed design duos such as Matey (interview, page 50) and John & Jane (interview, page 13), they reported they divvy up studio responsibilities based on each partner's individual strengths. At both studios, one partner focuses on managing the business side of things, while the other focuses on the creative design side. This does not have to be the split you use with your chosen partner, but you should divide tasks and labor that align with each of your unique talents. For instance, Josh Carnley from Matey credits these clear and defined roles as the key to working successfully together. He says about his partner (and wife) Shelton: "We knew she was really great at customer service. She's energetic and organized, so that's why she handles the business and account management. She gets new business, introduces our work to potential markets, and organizes projects from start to finish. We have a clean split in our roles, and I think that's what makes us work."

Developing a written agreement

Sometimes called a partnership agreement or an operating agreement, you need a document that outlines the details of how your business will be run. This agreement will require the two (or more) of you to set rules before you begin working together. As problems arise, you can return to this document to resolve them. Without an agreement in place, it will be harder to come to a resolution amid a stressful situation. If you struggle to come to a consensus now while creating this document, it might be a sign your partnership should not be pursued.

While this might seem like an overwhelming task, there are many resources to help you write a partnership agreement. Search in your local community for free or low-cost legal aid opportunities—for example, Lilian and I were able to work with a lawyer to develop ours as part of a business training program. There are also templates available online to assist in the development of your agreement. Here's a sample of some of the decisions you'll be making in advance:

- ***What are each of your individual responsibilities and roles in the business?*** This can outline your day-to-day tasks, such as how at Unsold Studio Lilian and I share the creative work, but I'm also responsible for writing project proposals and managing our finances. It might also describe more specialized responsibilities such as if anyone has the authority to take on business risks, for instance, applying for a bank loan or signing a lease on an office space.
- ***How do you each get paid and how much?*** Money can be one of the biggest stressors on a business partnership, so this is important. You do not necessarily have to receive the same cut of the profit just because you are partners. For example, since I take on the extra tasks outlined in the previous point, I receive a small percentage more to account for my additional time and labor.
- ***How much of the business do each of you own?*** Similarly, this might not necessarily be an equal split. If you are investing more in the business up front—say purchasing equipment or providing a workspace—should you own more of the business?
- ***If one of you decides to leave the business, what happens?*** This scenario can become complicated and has a lot of considerations. For instance, if one of you leaves, can the other still use the business name and its current brand identity? In the interview with Nuevo Studio (interview, page 132), owner Naoma told the story about how she initially had a different design business with a partner. When that partner suddenly decided to leave, based on their agreement, Naoma could not move forward with that current business. She had to start over from scratch. In your agreement, one option could be that the partner who wants to keep the business "buys out" the other partner. This is why setting ownership percentage matters. For example, if your partner owns 40 percent and decides they are done with the studio, you could pay them 40 percent of the total value of the studio to "buy them out." Then you would own 100 percent of the business, and they would be compensated for their efforts up to that point. If you include a "buy out" in your agreement, you might also want to include who you are able to sell your ownership stake to. For instance, in ours, we outline that we cannot sell to an outside person without us both agreeing. This means I cannot sell my ownership of Unsold Studio to someone random, and suddenly force Lilian to be partnered with them.
- ***If something unexpected happens—such as one of you gets sick or dies—what happens?*** I know this one is a downer, but the unexpected and unfortunate happens, and you have to be prepared. If one of you gets sick long term and cannot work, what's the protocol? If something worse happens, what happens to your ownership stake? For instance, if you have a spouse or child, would they become beneficiaries of your portion of the business?

- ***How do you handle conflicts if you do not agree on something?*** This is especially important if there is only two of you, and there's no obvious tiebreaker when you cannot come to a consensus. When Lilian and I worked with a lawyer to develop our agreement, he mentioned other clients bring in an agreed-upon outside person to cast a tiebreaking vote, while some flip a coin or play a game of "Rock, Paper, Scissors" to resolve their conflicts. While the last two might seem silly, they are legitimate if you both agree to that process.

If you still want to partner up, the two (or more) of you should go back to "Curate your online presence," in this chapter, if you have not done that yet. If you have, move on to "Find clients," later in this chapter, together. And if you decided to not partner up, keep moving forward solo!

Interview

John & Jane

Sarah Burley and Gareth Strange are the founders of John & Jane, a brand strategy and graphic design studio located in Barry, Vale of Glamorgan, Wales. The duo operates under the pseudonym John & Jane because they prefer the focus to be on their work, rather than on them. They selected it based on "John and Jane Doe," the well-known titles of anonymity. Funny enough, they are also their given middle names: Gareth *John* and Sarah *Jane*.

John & Jane's business strategy is to "just do good work." Sarah says, "We want to do the work, showcase the work, and then hopefully get more work." This ethos highlights their lack of ego, which can often feel like a rarity in an industry where many designers use their persona to sell services. Scrolling through John & Jane's website and social media accounts, you won't find many photographs featuring the designers; instead, they put their well-documented design work front and center. This approach underscores that they prioritize creating effective design for their clients rather than elevating their personal brand. What potential client wouldn't want to work with John & Jane based on that; a team who are humble, do great work, and put others first?

If you're someone who feels too shy to command a freelancing business, a common worry among my quieter students, let Sarah and Gareth serve as a way forward. These two have built a successful design studio while largely staying behind-the-scenes. However, they put themselves out there when it matters most—networking, speaking at conferences, and leading in their creative community—which I hope instills confidence that you can do it too.

Your path in design can be linear … or not

While Gareth and Sarah both worked in the design field prior to opening John & Jane, their stories are very different. Gareth, the Creative Director, had a more direct career path. He discovered design at a young age, and pursued a degree in graphic design at university. He worked in different agencies over the course of eight years, while doing illustrative work and small branding jobs on the side under the name "Strangelove." Sarah, the Strategy Director, had a more winding route. Out of university, she opened a sandwich shop with a friend. Even though that endeavor didn't last, she realized she liked owning a business. She then pursued her master of arts degree in literature, had a baby, began writing for different design agencies, and founded the Cardiff, Wales-based chapter of CreativeMornings, "a free monthly breakfast lecture series designed for creative communities."[3]

Their lives began to intertwine when they started working at an agency together. Soon after, Sarah pulled Gareth in to help her run CreativeMornings. Through these experiences, they realized their working relationship was "really fun, and we thought maybe we could do something on our own." They eventually went for it, and John & Jane was born.

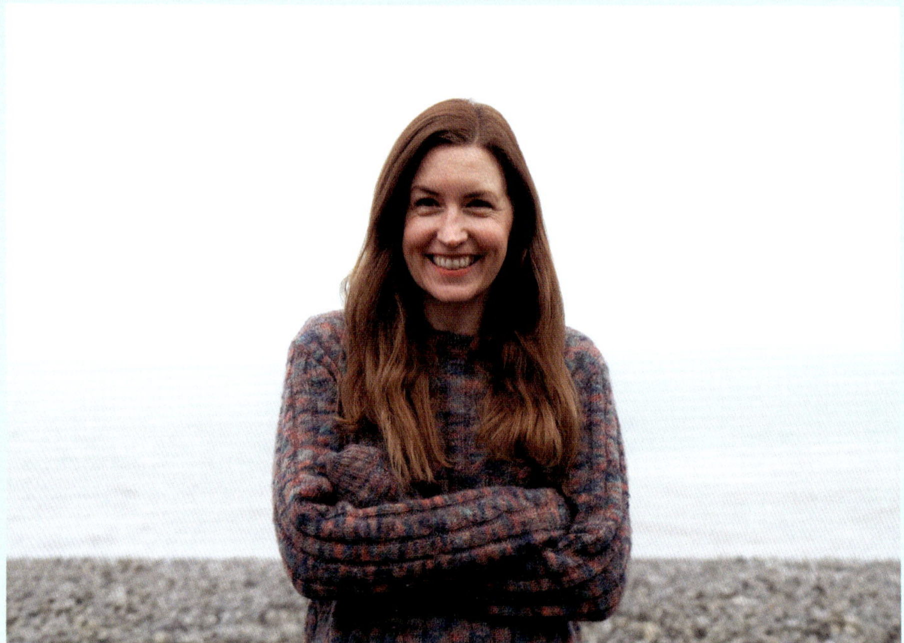

Figure 1.1 Sarah Burley of John & Jane. Image courtesy of John & Jane.

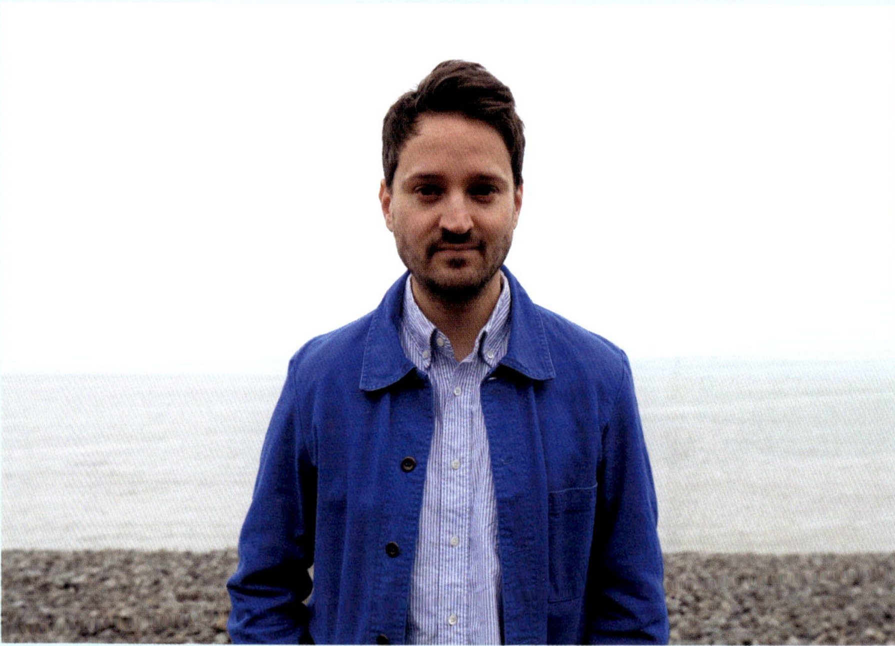

Figure 1.2 Gareth Strange of John & Jane. Image courtesy of John & Jane.

Create your own local network

CreativeMornings taught Sarah and Gareth they could work well together, but it also was fundamental to the success of their studio. Every month, a different theme is selected for the events that take place in 232 cities across sixty-eight countries.[4] By founding the Cardiff chapter of the organization, Sarah established herself as a creative leader in the community. Through her volunteer work running the group, she gave local creatives an opportunity to gather monthly and build their networks, including her own. "The power of the connections we made at CreativeMornings is so far reaching," Sarah says. For example, John & Jane sponsored one of the monthly lectures featuring one of their favorite printmakers. As part of the event, they had one hundred posters screen printed that promoted their studio. Gareth says, "The next thing you know, we had folks from established design agencies and universities Instagramming our poster on their walls." Through this seemingly simple gesture, more folks knew about John & Jane. "The very worst thing you can do if you freelance is isolate yourself and not be forming relationships with others." Every "first" client—regional, national, and international—for John & Jane has stemmed from a local connection such as CreativeMornings.

Sarah and Gareth's first design presentation as John & Jane was hyper-local: in their client's living room located a town away from their studio. They were presenting to a family-owned business called Prosecco Pronto, a mobile bar that delivers sparkling wine in a vintage Italian van. As a new design studio without a full roster of clients, Sarah and Gareth poured their time and energy into the project. Despite the small

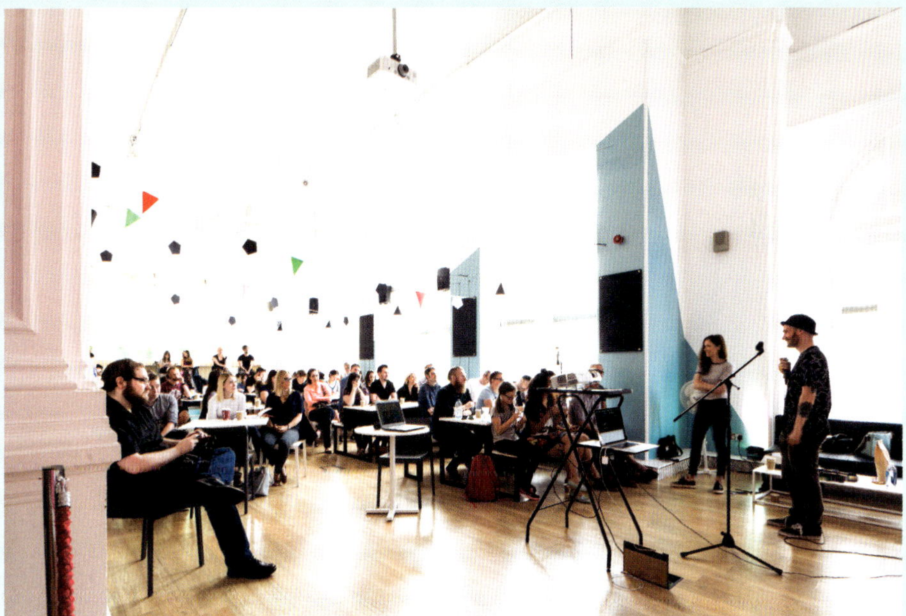

Figure 1.3 Gareth Strange giving a talk at CreativeMornings Cardiff on the theme of "Love" to their community in August 2016. Image courtesy of John & Jane.

budget, they knew the Prosecco Pronto opportunity could help establish them in their community as go-to designers. "We knew we could make the van design look distinctive and get a great portfolio piece, so we went above and beyond for the client. Sometimes you have to put in a little extra to build your business up and to gain experience, especially when you're just starting out."

Their experience with Prosecco Pronto garnered them more branding projects for food and beverage clients in the Cardiff area, such as the Grazing Shed and Tokyo Nights. The marketing manager for the two restaurants introduced them to their first national client: Princes Gate. The Wales-based mineral water company also had a hometown connection to Sarah: it's based where she grew up. She says, "It was a no brainer to take the project on," due to the personal connections to the client and the national reach it would bring them, despite another modest project budget. John & Jane's brand refresh for the bottled water included a new website and strategy, which emphasized Princes Gate's good environmental practices and production methods. They also leaned into making the brand "Welsh and proud," as it's filtered by the rocks of Wales, but is also an official partner with the Welsh Rugby Union and Football Association of Wales.

Their first international client Rubrik, a US-based start-up, was introduced to them by a childhood classmate of Gareth's. He'd even played football (soccer to Americans like me) with her dad at the local football club, Cwmbran Celtic. "We might have been the only designers she knew," Gareth laughs about how they were hired.

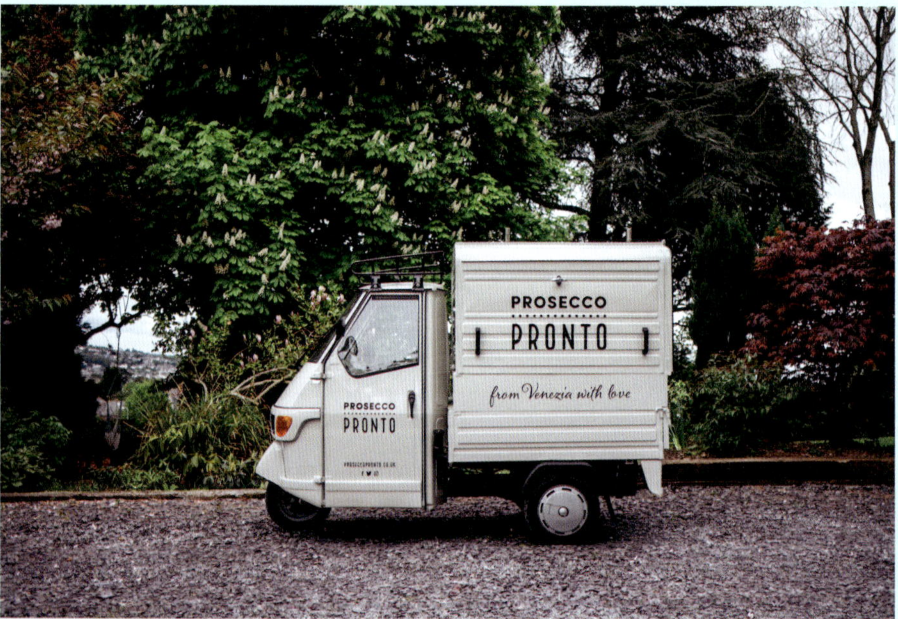

Figure 1.4 Starting small, literally! One of their first projects was providing a small family-run business with a classic, practical, and highly usable brand for Prosecco Pronto. Image courtesy of John & Jane.

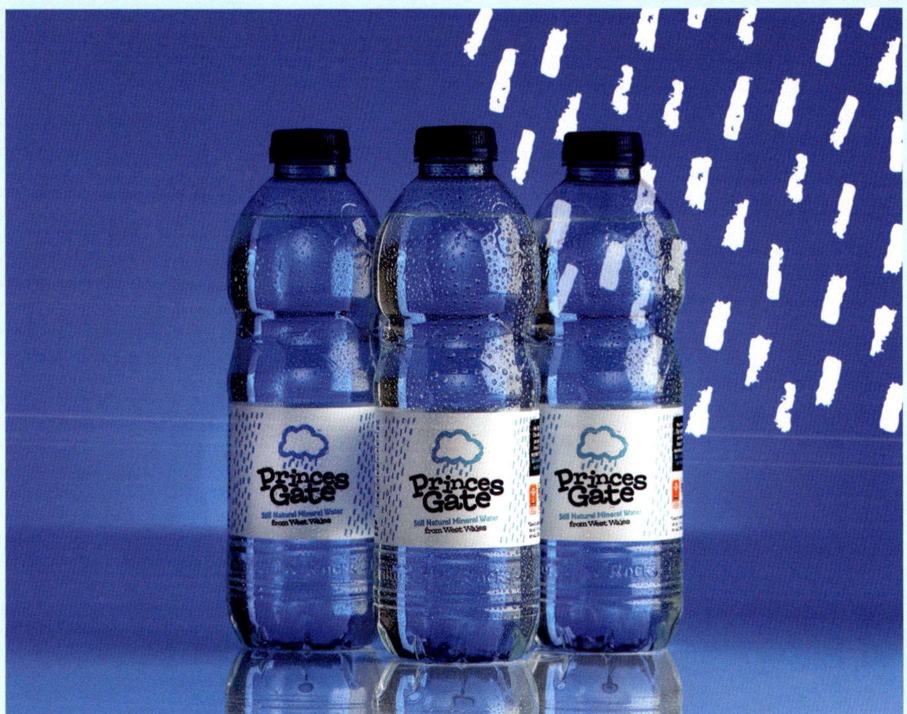

Figure 1.5 The newly designed bottle labels for Wales-based Princes Gate mineral water by John & Jane. Image courtesy of John & Jane.

"We started with some tiny projects like icon designs for her," Gareth continued. Soon after, those small projects led to bigger projects, with John & Jane now leading their big brand campaigns and events, such as the Forward Digital Summit and to promote Rubrik's partnership with Mercedes-AMG Petronas Motorsport.

Gareth notes, "Whatever project you get, go for it 100%. Even if you have a dry brief, you can make it creative. You never know where that client might go, or who they'll talk to. I did design work for a friend when I was nineteen for free, and years later, they connected us to bigger opportunities that paid. It all comes back around."

Become a design partner in your community

Even though John & Jane's client list has gone global, they continue to work in their neighborhood. Sarah says, "We always have local projects going on. We have close relationships with these clients, and we want to see them succeed. Because of the physical proximity, we get the chance to see the results of our work together and it's very rewarding."

Many of the nearby clients John & Jane align themselves with aim to better their community, such as One Twelve Coffee. The Newport, Wales-based client is "a nonprofit coffee shop that invests in people who have experienced homelessness, helping them to get back into housing, work, and society." An initiative of the Pobl Housing Group, the shop provides a barista training program for their tenants to help build skills and confidence that encourages independence. Gareth cites the project as one he's most proud to have been a part of, through naming and creating the brand identity. Sarah says, "We believe in the power of branding and its ability to improve lives in the right hands."

This is not the only project John & Jane has done for housing associations such as the Pobl Group. "We've basically worked with almost every housing association in South Wales. Now, we've rebranded four of them and done little projects for many others. We love how they look after the community, and often fill in the gaps of where the government may be letting people down in terms of services." They acquired this type of work by speaking at various housing conferences in Wales. "It can be quite scary to get out of your comfort zone and speak, especially to people in a completely different industry." Sarah and Gareth had attended design-centered events, which were helpful, but found more success landing clients by attending conferences outside of their field. "For people working in housing or other non-design jobs, it can be hard to find a good design partner. By speaking at their events, we made it easy for them to find us and understand why they might need us."

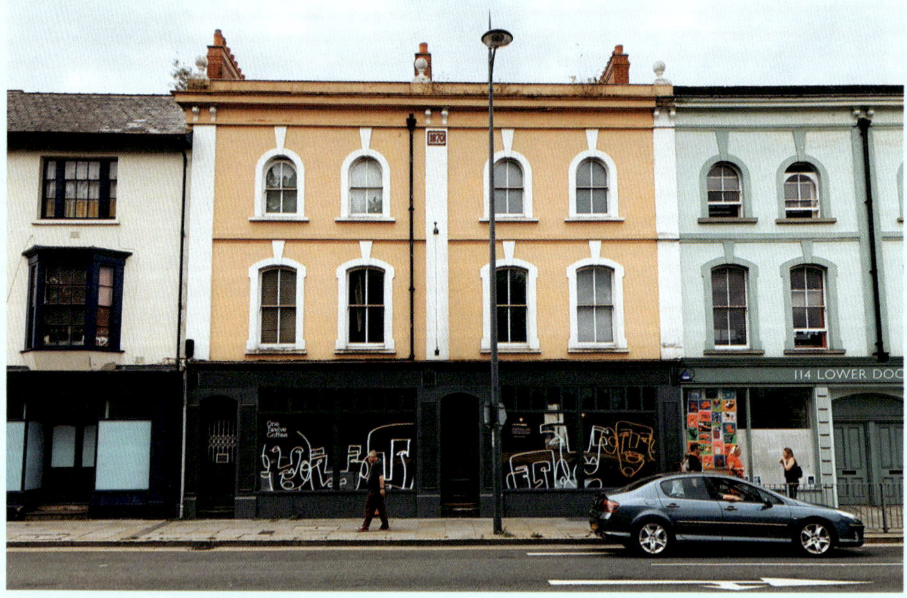

Figure 1.6 John & Jane used the One Twelve Coffee Illustrations they designed to create an abstract, welcoming, and fun window design in the neighborhood. Image courtesy of John & Jane.

Set boundaries

John & Jane succeeds because of the chemistry between Sarah and Gareth. They admit, "it can be hard to find someone to work with like this, and we're really lucky." While they have hired employees to help them in the studio in the past, they admit when it's only the two of them, "it feels easier. We always know where we are."

Having separate areas of expertise has created an effective workflow in their studio and helps resolve disagreements when they arise during the creative process. Sarah says,

> **I do the strategy side of things, including discovery, content, and copy. Gareth leads the visuals and graphic design. We discuss elements of each project, and if there's a difference of opinion about something along the way, we respect one another. If we disagree on logos or colors, he ultimately gets the final say, whereas I'll get the last word if we argue about things in my area.**

Their best advice for working with a loved one or friend is to "remember to keep it professional. You have to be respectful and can't bring in any baggage from your relationship outside the studio into work."

Sarah and Gareth admit they're in their studio a lot, but it is important that "the work doesn't swallow everything else up and take over your entire life. It can be hard to set boundaries around when you will work because you can't predict when you'll be feeling creative." They recommend once you have the luxury to turn down projects, do so as a way to conserve your energy. "We often said yes to work because we didn't want to let people down or not work with them. Over time, we've learned to be more realistic and say no for the sake of our current clients, the quality of our work, and our sanity."

To learn more about Sarah, Gareth and John & Jane:

johnandjane.agency

@john8jane

Find clients

You cannot wait for a design project to fall in your lap. You must be proactive in pursuing client work. Sometimes you have to create the opportunity by dreaming it up and offering it to someone.

It took Unsold Studio about three years until we were not consistently hustling for design work. Eventually, potential clients were coming to us because our client base and reputation had grown. However, we never take our stream of design work for granted—we still have slow periods where I need to tap into these different groups—my personal network, fellow designers, and my local community—to drum up projects.

Shamelessly tell everyone

Tell everyone, I mean *everyone*, that you're a designer and you're taking on clients. You never know who or where work will come from. Do not keep your freelancing dreams a secret. While this may feel cringy, especially if you're shy, think of it like you're flipping your store's sign from closed to open, or turning on your taxi's light. You must signal to others that you're pursuing client work, so they perceive you as a hirable design resource.

Illustrator Courtney Jentzen said when she decided to freelance full-time, she emailed everyone in her contact list. This included family and friends, but also former colleagues and clients from her previous design positions. Here's what she shamelessly sent on April 16, 2010:

Hey everyone!

I wanted to share with you that after many months of hard work I am officially announcing the launch of my very own business, Swiss Cottage Designs.

Swiss Cottage Designs was born this past September when I left my full-time job to pursue my own dream. I am a custom design studio specializing in everything from wedding and party invites to baby announcements, custom illustrations and pretty much anything else in between. While the website is still under construction, I have my blog for you all to check out.

Owning a business has always been something that I wanted to do. My parents can attest that by the age of 10 I had a babysitting agency, a dog walking company and was running a summer day camp program. I think I was meant to do this.

The best way for any small business to grow is by word of mouth and referrals. Please feel free to send this to any of your friends and family members if you think they'd be interested. I am open for business and I couldn't be more excited!

Thanks guys,
Courtney
www.swisscottagedesigns.com

Even if you're not ready to quit your day job and freelance full-time, you can use Courtney's example as a template to announce that you're beginning to take on occasional design projects.

When I asked Courtney why she sent this message, she said,

> *I knew that if everyone I was connected with knew what I was doing, they'd tell their networks and advocate for me. After I sent that email, my friend's parent's friend who owned an x-ray business reached out for business card designs. My other friend's dad was a volunteer for a jazz festival, so they recommended me to create flyers for the event. These projects may seem small, but they made me feel productive and energized. Those early projects led to more projects, like a ripple effect, and it started with that email blast.*

Similarly, when designer Alessandra Corbett (interview, page 32) was looking for freelance work, she "went into overdrive." She said, "I made postcards advertising my studio and sent those out. I sent emails to people I barely knew offering my design services. I went on Instagram and started following people and commenting, creating work and sharing work to try to get noticed. I put everything into trying to make freelancing happen for me."

By announcing to your immediate connections, whether that's through emails, social media posts, tangible items such as postcards, or in-person conversations, you're expanding your reach for potential projects. Once folks know you're a designer, especially one that is actively seeking freelance work, they will become your unofficial public relations team. While someone may not personally have design work for you, they will happily recommend you to people in their networks who do, helping you cast a much wider net. Recently, when someone approached Unsold Studio for an opportunity, I asked them how they heard about us. Turns out, a woman I'd chatted with years before was the recommender. In that single casual conversation, I'd shared my design story with her and in turn the woman had become my cheerleader without me even realizing it.

While it can seem scary to publicly open yourself up this way, most people will greet you with positivity. And if they don't, they're jerks—forget about them. You wouldn't want to work with them anyway. If this all still seems intimidating, head to "How to talk to strangers" later in this chapter to build some confidence.

I'll break down how to specifically target various groups to acquire freelance projects ahead—"Personal network" (page 22), "Fellow designers" (page 23), and "Local community" (page 25)—but for now, seize every opportunity to share that you're a designer without shame.

Personal network

I recommend starting here, with people you know and feel comfortable with. Look for "low-stakes work"; the friend who has a band and needs merch designed, your uncle who needs a better sign for the craft fair, or your sister who wants to start a YouTube channel. In the beginning, these projects might be unsolicited by your loved ones. Instead, you offer your design services to help them for no- or low-cost. While I do not advocate for doing free or discounted work forever, in the beginning, it can be good to do this within your personal network. These types of people are apt to be patient as you hone your freelancing process because they care about you (and because they aren't paying you much). You'll benefit by helping a family member or friend; a win-win.

Our first Unsold Studio project came from my summer waitressing gig. One day, my manager and friend, told me that he dreamed of being a chef and opening his own restaurant someday. After tasting his food and doing a little thinking, I offered to help him make it a reality. I pitched that I would brand his food business, then create a website where people could buy tickets for a pop-up dinner in a mystery location (which turned out to be my loft apartment). We agreed that I would do this work for free, but he would pay me back once his business became profitable. While it was a risk that I might never get paid for my labor, at that time, I needed the client experience more than I needed the extra cash.

From there, I worked with him to name the business, create the brand identity, launch the website, design the menus, set the table, host the guests in my space, and wash dishes after they left—I half-joke it was the most dedicated I've ever been to a client. However, it was rewarding to see my design work help my chef friend take off. The first dinner we hosted, it was all his family and friends. Then the next dinner, still mostly family and friends, with a handful of strangers. Eventually, we didn't know anyone in the room. He started to get invited to host pop-up dinners throughout Detroit, to cater for events, and he was able to launch his own food truck. With his popularity rising, so did ours. We were able to say we'd done the design work for his then well-known food business, which gave us credibility when approaching prospective clients. It was a favorable situation for all of us.

My chef friend also became a champion for our design business. After our work helped him, he started our word-of-mouth business; he recommended our services to his friends who needed a brand identity for their real estate company. Their project, which we eventually landed, was our first experience freelancing for people we didn't know directly. From that project, came more projects.

This is a common pattern for new business growth. Offering your services to your family and friends is like dropping a stone in water. Soon after impact, there's a ripple effect that expands your business to their networks and beyond. This trajectory happened to both my chef friend and me, and it can to you too. Seek out people in your life with potential projects that you can use as a catalyst for your freelancing work. Think about individual people, but also the groups you belong to—athletic teams, religious communities, book clubs, and so on. There's definitely an untapped design opportunity somewhere in your life right now.

Head to "Special 'first date' considerations," in Chapter 2, for more information about how best to work with people you're close to.

Fellow designers

The perception is that the design field is competitive, which it is, but it can also be generous. Often designers will share work with other designers, so having friends in the industry will provide project leads. Designers share work when:

- ***They cannot take the project on.*** The project is not a good fit for them, but it might be for you. If you befriend designers who are ahead of you career-wise, you can often receive project "run-off." Designer Naoma Serna-Zahn from Nuevo Studio (interview, page 132) said,

  > *I get a lot of potential clients that come to me, and they're not a good fit because of the budget or whatever it may be, but it's a really great fit for a new freelancer. A $2,000 project might not be worth me taking on, but it is for them. You should know the people in your industry because a lot of jobs and opportunities pop up like this, and other designers will recommend you if you make a good impression.*

- ***They need extra hands on a project.*** Designers will sometimes hire independent contractors, namely, freelancers, to work for them on a project-by-project basis. This is called *"sub-contracting"—when an individual or company hires someone outside of their team to fulfill part or all their duties on a specific project.* While the other designer will primarily get the credit for the work you complete, this can be a great way to gain experience, make money, and receive mentorship from a more senior designer. If you decide to go down this route, be sure you understand the terms and conditions of working for that designer.
- ***They have outgrown the client.*** As designers grow their businesses, things change. For example, when Unsold Studio began, we were willing to work all hours of the day and night for our clients. Over time, our priorities have shifted. We no longer want to offer that level of on-demand service. However, some of our early clients expected that because they had always received it from us. When we tried to pull back our working hours, it created tension and resentment with some of those clients—we were no longer a good fit for one another. Our solution was to redirect them to other designers, often emerging ones such as yourself, who were willing to put in longer hours to get their businesses off the ground.
- ***They are in a different design field.*** As graphic designers, we often receive recommendations from connections in the architecture or interior design fields because their client needs a brand identity or environmental graphics.

We return the favor and recommend photographers, illustrators, and developers to our clients who are looking for those types of services. Since we're not in direct competition with each other, sharing work and clients comes with less baggage. With many projects requiring more than one type of creative expertise, make friends with other types of designers.

Where to find other designers

Established design networks

There are many design organizations that have active communities for you to plug into. These groups regularly host events, both in-person and online, where you can meet other creative people. What's great about these organizations is that networking is a clear goal for participants, making it less awkward to introduce yourself to a stranger.

Below I've listed a few types of design networks to look for but do some research to see what will be the best fit for you. Once you've found the right network(s) for you, be sure to sign-up for their mailing list and follow them on social media to stay up to date on their goings-on.

- Professional organizations for specific design fields, such as the AIGA (American Institute of Graphic Arts)—the professional association for design, which attracts primarily communication designers.
- Design groups that are inclusive of many creative fields, such as CreativeMornings, which you can learn about in the interview with John & Jane (page 13).
- Identity-based designer communities, such as Ladies, Wine, & Design and Organization for Black Designers.
- Location-specific design networks, for instance, UNESCO Creative Cities Network, which is how I met OuterEdit (interview, page 107).

"Cold call"

This term comes from when people would actually call someone on the phone. However, you can say cold email, text, or direct message these days. The important bit is "cold"; *it means that you are reaching out to someone you have not interacted with before to generate project leads*. If there are designers or studios you admire, send them a cold something, to introduce yourself. I've met many fellow designers, such as my friend Courtney, who I've mentioned a few times, this way. A "cold call" can seem intimidating, but in reality, the worst thing that happens is the person doesn't respond or says "no." I guarantee you've been ignored or been told "no" before. You survived then, and you'll survive again.

In these "cold calls" with other designers, it's important to:

- ***Personalize the message.*** This should not read like you copy and pasted the same message to 100 other designers. You can use a template to make these reach-outs easier but be sure that the person on the other end feels like you are speaking specifically to them, for instance, mention a particular project from their portfolio.

- ***Make it easy for the person on the other end.*** If you are sending a general introduction email, that's okay, but having a clear request will incentivize the person to respond (for better or for worse). Assume the person you're trying to connect with is busy. Keep your ask simple, and make it easy for them to complete the request: Do you want to have a quick coffee over Zoom with them? List your availability in the coming weeks in your initial message.

  If you're a student or recent graduate, seasoned designers are often very giving of their time to you at this stage; they remember how hard it was starting out. Do not be afraid to mention that you're an emerging designer. Consider approaching them as a potential mentor, asking to interview them about their career, a portfolio review, or for a studio visit.
- ***Think of this like planting the seeds of a relationship, not selling your services outright.*** You'll notice in the examples above, neither asked the person to pass along client work or to reveal their project pricing structure It can feel presumptuous to go into your first interaction with someone with those sorts of requests. Instead, try to form an authentic relationship with them that you'll build slowly over time.

See "Special 'first date' considerations," in Chapter 2, for more information about how to best work with other designers.

Local community

No matter where you live, there are potential clients—I promise. The mom-and-pop shops, school groups, restaurants, places of worship, libraries, event organizers, charities, farms, bands, clubs, government entities, sports teams, theater troupes, nonprofits, and more that make up your community all have design needs. Often small businesses and community organizations do not have the ability to hire an in-house designer due to cost constraints and a lack of consistent day-to-day design needs. This means when design opportunities arise, they likely look outside to free-lancers like you to help accomplish their goals.

Other local groups may never have worked with a designer before, which is some-times unfortunately very apparent (think ineffective promotional materials, illegible signage, hard-to-navigate menus). While it might be tempting in these scenarios to say to the local pizza shop owner, "I'd love to redesign your menu because it's so terrible and *really* ugly," you have to go into these situations with tact. For many small businesses and organizations, design is perceived as an "extra" rather than an essential. Your challenge will be pitching your design services as a wise business investment that will solve problems for whomever you're approaching. Luckily, it's been proven that design has a positive economic impact.

A study by McKinsey & Company in 2018, called the *Business Value of Design*,[5] found that companies they identified as top design performers increased revenue and shareholder returns at nearly twice the rate as their industry counterparts. While the McKinsey study looked at 300 publicly listed companies, and your neigh-borhood businesses are likely not worried about the stock market and shareholders, the findings suggest that "good design matters and the market rewards those who implement it."

While you might never have dreamed of designing for these kinds of small-scale local clients, such as the auto mechanic or dry cleaner down the street, they are perfect for beginner freelancers due to their manageable sizes and budgets. As a member of their community, you will better understand their goals, their challenges, and their audience(s). By working with these types of clients, you'll empower your neighborhood through design while gaining valuable freelancing experience.

Where to find non-designers in your community

Nonprofits and volunteer-based groups

When you're looking for your first clients, these types of groups are perfect "low-stakes" projects. Normally, nonprofits are operating on grant funding and volunteer labor. Instead of helping in more traditional roles, you can "give back" using your design skills. For instance, instead of walking dogs at the local animal shelter, you could offer to design adoption materials or create a brand identity for their upcoming fundraiser. This type of *volunteer-based work for the public good is often referred to as "pro bono"* or an "in-kind donation."

While these will likely be low- or no-pay projects, there are other types of benefits, such as:

- You'll gain client experience while making a positive impact, especially for those who need it the most in your community.
- You can select the opportunities that align with your values, interests, and goals. For example, if you care about veterans, work with a group dedicated to them. If your dream is designing for film and television, volunteer to create promotional materials for your community theater's upcoming production.
- If the client is not monetarily invested (paying you for the work), they will potentially be lower maintenance throughout the project. They might be more flexible with timelines, less demanding in their feedback, and express gratitude throughout the experience that makes you feel valued.
- There may be a tax benefit for donating your design services to a non-profit depending on where you live. Ask the client and/or speak with a tax specialist to learn more.

My first unpaid community-based project was one of the most meaningful of my career. As a design student, I interned for Big Duck, a Brooklyn, New York-based company that solely worked with nonprofits. At the time, this felt very uncool as my friends were interning at places such as television channels, fashion magazines, and flashy advertising studios. In reality, these friends were doing grunt work, for instance, delivering coffees and running errands. However, at my internship, I was assigned to lead my own design project for a real client: rebranding a local preschool.

While thankful for the opportunity, I was not excited to brag about it with my hip art school friends when I got back to campus. However, when I later presented my design solution to the preschool director, she teared up. She said something along the lines of, "I'm excited that my students and their families will be proud to come to school every day. Our sign and our brand finally will reflect who we are as a community." I felt an immense sense of pride. Seeing her emotional response made me understand how powerful my design skills could be, especially when directed toward a good cause. Most importantly, it taught me that "uncool" or "unsexy" work is often the most rewarding. By taking on a project with a local nonprofit or community group, my hope is you'll learn what I did first-hand, on top of gaining practical freelancing experience.

Established business networks

Most communities, even small towns, have hubs for business owners and entrepreneurs. These groups offer valuable resources that enhance the surrounding business community. By joining, you'll form relationships with a host of folks who are actively working to improve their companies and collaborate with others. Your freelancing will also benefit from their general business programming. Networking is expected in these groups, so no need to be shy. Look for:

- local government-based groups such as chambers of commerce
- small business associations
- neighborhood-specific business associations
- business and start-up incubators
- local economy-focused clubs
- business coaches and educators
- co-working spaces

Some of these business networks offer programming for their members—you could offer to give a presentation or workshop about your field of design, educating attendees about how you could improve their businesses. These types of events allow you to pitch your design services to a room of new people. Lilian and I have given these types of talks before, and they usually result in project leads from the attendees.

A term you might hear while you're hanging out with these groups is *"RFP," which stands for "Request for Proposal."* Some businesses and organizations will post a RFP—sometimes publicly on their website and sometimes more privately in select networks- which is *a document that outlines a project they're looking to have designed.* They're literally requesting that you propose to do their project. See Figure 1.7 for a sample RFP.

If you're interested in the project, you submit an application, that is, a project proposal, which I outline how to develop in Chapter 3, "If you want to pursue the project." All interested designers submit their proposals by the posted RFP deadline, and the client will hire a designer from the pool of submissions.

RFP SAMPLE

NOTES:

REQUEST FOR PROPOSAL
Bales' Botanicals / Perfume Brand

ABOUT THE PROJECT
Bales' Botanicals is a family-owned florist expanding its business from bouquets to perfumes. Their new product line will include four different scents. The client wants the brand to communicate the organic ingredients, be gender inclusive, and embrace its small business roots.

DELIVERABLES
- Brand Name
- Brand Identity System (logo, typefaces, colors, etc.)
- Bottle Label Designs (4)

TIMELINE
Bottle Label Designs (4) must be sent to production within three months of RFP deadline.

BUDGET
$4,000

QUESTION PERIOD
One week before the deadline, the client will host a video conference call to answer any RFP questions in a public forum. Register for the event here.

DUE DATE
29 December 2024 / hola@balesbotanicals.com

HERE'S AN EXAMPLE OF AN RFP. Yes, sometimes these documents are this scarce with information and include potentially unrealistic expectations. What information or follow-up questions would you have for the client in their scheduled public forum? For example, I'd want to know if the budget is solely the designer's fee or if that also includes production costs for the bottle label designs?

After you read Chapter 3, "If you want to pursue the project," challenge yourself to develop a proposal based on this sample RFP.

Figure 1.7 RFP sample and exercise.

While RFPs can be an avenue to acquire clients and projects, they can be "riskier" than other methods. This is because:

- Writing proposals is an unpaid form of labor—there is no guarantee you'll land the job. In most scenarios, you chat with a potential client to learn about the project before officially proposing to work together. This allows you to gather information directly from them, asking questions and follow-ups as needed. From that dialogue, you can determine if the project is a good fit and, if it is, develop a proposal.
  However, with RFPs, there is no back-and-forth discussion between you and the potential client. Instead, the information is pre-prepared by the client and presented to you in written form. The issue is that not all RFPs contain a standard set of information; some will provide ample project details, while others are vague and leave out necessary information. Others are not written by someone familiar with the design process, so project timelines and budgets seem unreasonable for what is being requested. In the "normal" potential client scenario, you'd be able to ask them if they're flexible on the timeline, but with an RFP, you have to decide if you'll stick to their very tight timeline or risk proposing a more reasonable one. Occasionally RFP processes will include a forum where you can ask clarifying questions before submitting your proposal, but not always.
  Each RFP will detail a unique selection process with varying requirements. With every RFP being so different from one another, you have to comb through each document carefully to create an accurate and competitive project proposal, which can be extremely time consuming. This time investment might be worth it if you get hired for the project, but if you don't … maybe not.
- With RFPs, sometimes it feels like you're shouting into the void when you submit your proposal. Often, you have not met, seen, or spoken to the person on the receiving end of an RFP at that stage. The anonymity of the RFP process diminishes your best sales tool: you. I'm confident people will always hire the designer with the decent portfolio who they feel a positive connection with, rather than the designer with the exceptional portfolio who rubs them the wrong way. You also miss out on the opportunity to see if the potential client is a good fit *for you*—do they seem like someone you want to work with? This is why networking and speaking to folks is so important, and why RFPs can be less fruitful than other methods to attract clients.

While I might seem negative about RFPs, our studio has acquired some great projects and clients through this process. We've also been flat out rejected too. Submitting for RFPs will become easier once you have more proposal writing and client experience. You'll become more confident in your design process, better equipped to interpret the client's requests, and be more efficient writing proposals. However, if a great RFP comes your way before then, go for it—just weigh the "risks" before you submit!

"Cold call"

Expanding your network in your local community through "cold calls" is a great strategy to find more freelancing work. Many small businesses and organizations in your neighborhood are open to the public, so your "cold calling" can include walking into their shop or attending one of their events. This is unlike "cold calling" other designers, whose workspaces are typically private, which forces you to email or message them. As many of us know, those types of online communications are easy to ignore. However, it's harder to ignore someone who is standing in front of you and introducing themselves. This is why I recommend trying to have your local community "cold calls" be in-person if possible.

If this makes you feel nervous, start with a local business you're already a patron of. This will make your "cold call" feel more like a "lukewarm call." As their customer, you already have an advantage—you'll know what they offer, understand their audience because you're a part of it, and can identify some possible design needs they have. For example, my husband and I frequently shop at a garden store in our neighborhood. Soon after launching Unsold Studio, I went in to buy some plants and soil. I made a point to finally introduce myself to the employee that often helped me, but I did not personally know. In that conversation, I asked if they were planning to add online ordering to their website in the future. Since I had shopped with them before, I already knew they did not offer any e-commerce. I also knew that their website lacked the charm of their in-person greenhouse experience. However, I posed the question neutrally without giving my opinion of the site. This way, I would not hurt anyone's feelings, but it would still give me the opportunity to sneak in that I was a local designer and if they ever needed help with their site, I lived right around the corner. I left my business card with the employee and went about my day. Soon after, the business owner connected with me. I feel like because I was a familiar face around their shop, it made them feel more comfortable reaching out to me to discuss what we could offer them. Eventually, they hired us to refresh their site.

See "Special 'first date' considerations," in Chapter 2, for more information about how best to work with folks in your community you are not familiar with.

How to talk to strangers

My students often tell me the term "networking" is fear-inducing. If you're like them and the idea of talking to strangers makes you sweaty, this section is for you. There's ample research and tips to improve your social skills that you can look into, but here's a few ways to help alleviate stress as you expand your circle:

Ask yourself, "What's the worst that could happen?"

As creatives, we have big imaginations and can easily dream up wild, and highly unlikely, scenarios about what could go wrong in social situations. When I'm worried about approaching someone new, I ask myself "What's the worst that could happen?" After rotating through every outlandish possibility, I remember that no matter what I do or say, I cannot control the other person's response. If it turns out the person is a jerk—someone that makes you feel less than, laughs at you, ignores you, or rejects you—you wouldn't want to be associated with them anyway. With this logic, the worst that can happen is that you'll quickly learn the person is not a good fit for you and your goals, which actually seems like a win to me.

Have a go-to conversation entry point, then follow-up with questions

There are lots of tactics to start talking with someone new, but my favorite is to break the ice with a compliment. This starts your interaction on a positive note and is an easy way to get the other person's attention. Once you have that, keep the conversation going by asking the other person questions about themselves: *this is the key to small talk*. I find the majority of people like to speak about themselves, whether they admit it or not. By asking someone thoughtful questions and actively listening, you make the other person feel seen and heard. Who wouldn't want to be around someone who makes them feel that way?

Remember everyone's awkward sometimes

You're not the only person who is naturally shy, a little clumsy around strangers, or afraid of small talk. In new social settings, most people feel self-conscious; some people are just better at hiding it. If you're nervous, it's okay to acknowledge it to the person you're talking to. By saying it out loud, I'm convinced you take away the power of your nerves. Since that feeling is so human, I bet the other person will empathize with you. In my experience, most people are kind and willing to help if they know you're struggling. In this scenario, they might tell a joke to make you feel lighter, take charge of the conversation to take the pressure off you, or introduce you to other people to make sure you feel included. If the situation were reversed, where someone confided in you that they were a little uneasy around new people, I guarantee you'd try to make them feel comfortable. Trust that strangers, even if they seem intimidating, are probably just as nervous, and as nice, as you. And if they're not, go back to my first point—they're not worth your time.

End a good conversation with the ability to pick it up again

Remember that networking is not about instant gratification. It's highly unlikely you'll chat with someone once, then they hire you on the spot for a project. Introducing yourself to someone is like planting the seed of a relationship. You have to tend to it, otherwise it will not grow and produce fruit.

If you feel like you had a productive interaction with someone new, wrap up the chat by saying something like, "It's been so great to meet you. Do you have a business card or a social media account I could follow? I'd love to stay up to date on what you're working on." This gives you a way to stay connected with them later. If they oblige, follow through and check in with them once in a while. You do not need to become their number one fan, but here and there send them a message to ask how they're doing. By continuing to positively and authentically engage with them, you'll remain active in their minds and likelier to benefit from all that networking.

Interview

The Homegrown Studio

Alessandra Corbett is the founder and art director of The Homegrown Studio, a brand design and creative marketing team freelancing for small businesses, farms, and community organizations.

For me, her story is extra special: I grew up in a small town not far from where Alessandra lives and works. As a young adult, I felt like I had to move to an urban area to "make it" as a designer. When home on summer break from college in New York City, a mentor encouraged me to build a design business in my rural hometown once I graduated, but I could not envision it. Years later when I discovered The Homegrown Studio, I finally saw what my mentor had. Frankly, I felt a pang of jealousy for what Alessandra built and sadness for what I'd missed out on.

Alessandra's work is beautiful, but more importantly, it uplifts her community through design. Examples in her portfolio such as the Wilbraham Welcome Project cultivate a sense of pride to be from a small town and to be "filled with local love." I moved away from my hometown as soon as I could, but I wonder if design work such as Alessandra's had existed whether I would have been a "proud townie" instead. Her portfolio and story serve as a testament that you can build a successful design career anywhere, even your small farm town, and that you can use your design skills to create the community you want to belong to.

Start with what you know

Alessandra found her first clients at the local farmers market, a community she knows well: her family owns and operates a farm in town. While shopping the booths, she noticed many of the agriculture businesses did not have logos or marketing materials to help their products stand out. Soon after, Alessandra began passing out business cards and brochures to offer her design services to the vendors.

She acquired one farmers market client, then another and another, until vendors and farms were reaching out to her organically (pun intended) to hire her to design for them. At that time, she focused on creating a niche client base by concentrating on small businesses that came from the markets, and she leaned into her agricultural knowledge and aesthetic. "The work I do for farms and local agriculture is so important to me. It's in my roots, and I'm super excited anytime I can collaborate with anyone tending to the land." Her portfolio grew to include clients across the United States' northeast such as Bell Brook Farm, Chase Hill Farm, Thomas Farm & Dairy, Rooted Flowers, Diemand Farm, Woven Stars Farm, Little Farmhouse Flowers, and von Trapp Flowers.

"It's such a neat feeling when I go into the grocery store and I see products like Thomas Farm & Dairy's goat cheeses." The farm is known for its award-winning cheeses, and the labels and branding Alessandra created for them have likewise been recognized as award-winning. She notes,

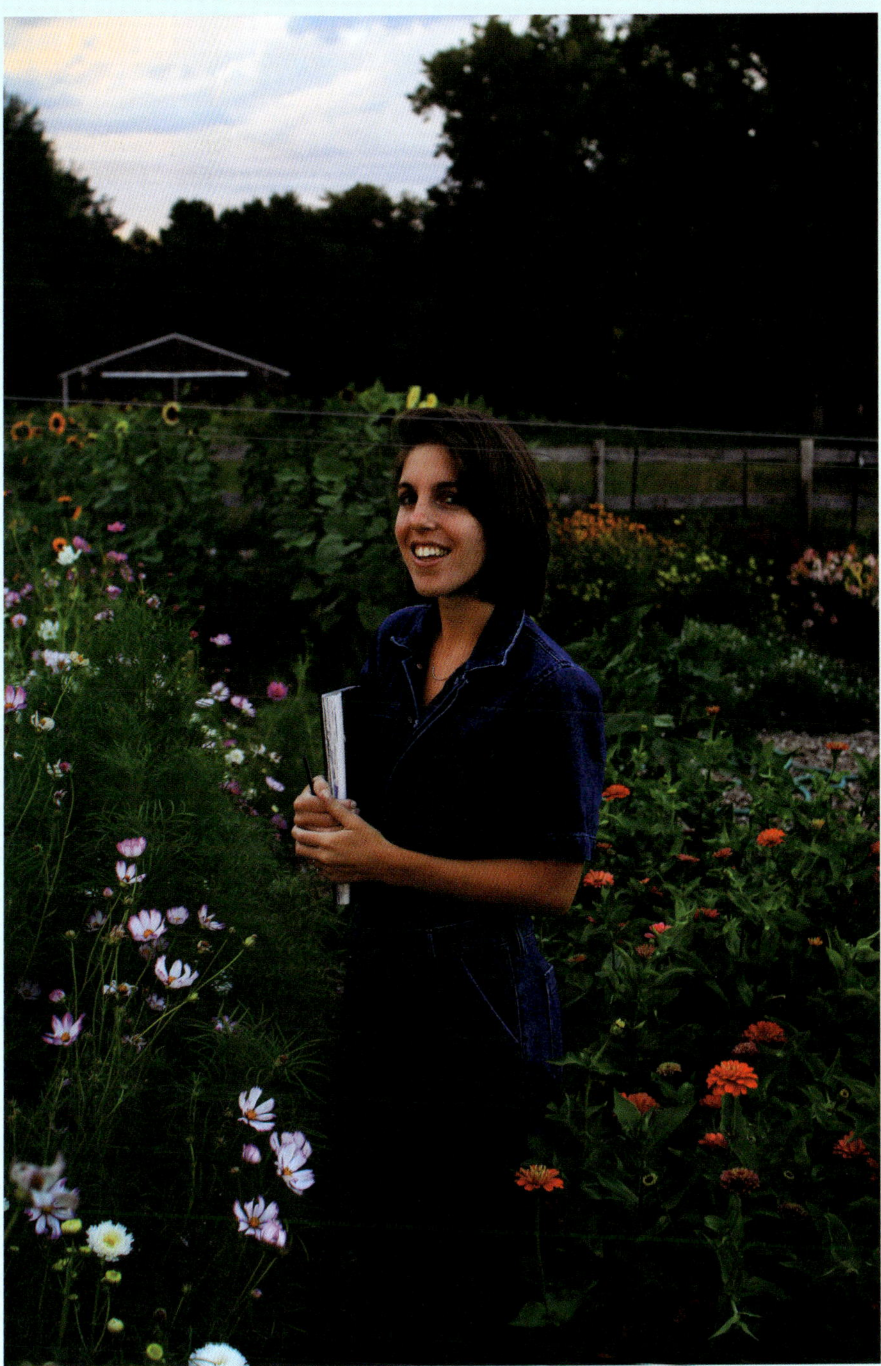

Figure 1.8 Alessandra Corbett of The Homegrown Studio. Image courtesy of The Homegrown Studio.

> **Of course it's cool to see your own design work out there in the real world, but even better is witnessing the tangible difference it can make for these small businesses. Before the big rebrand for Thomas Farm & Dairy, it was a challenge to pick out their cheeses among a sea of similar labels. Now, these cheeses really carry some shelf presence and are able to clearly differentiate from their competitors, which gets more eyes on the amazing work the dairy is doing—and certainly results in more sales! Seeing that positive difference design can ignite in my clients' businesses is what really excites me. When those businesses succeed, our community succeeds as a whole, and I'm really happy I can play a part in that development.**

Exiting a full-time job for freelancing

While designing for her farm clients, Alessandra was still working full-time in marketing at a company that manufactured and sold horse care products internationally.

> **That first job out of college was an excellent education in how a business operates. I learned a lot about marketing, but I was bored creatively, which can happen at in-house roles. Freelancing on the side allowed me to use my creativity in different ways, on a scale that was less corporate and structured than my day job. It was refreshing and exciting to imagine the possibilities.**

Her freelancing projects were piling up when a local nonprofit organization, Community Involved in Sustaining Agriculture (CISA), contacted her with a proposal to partner with them in assisting local farms with branding through grant opportunities. This type of work would provide a more consistent revenue stream for Alessandra, and she was excited about beginning the collaboration with CISA. However, the same week she began that work, her full-time job laid her off.

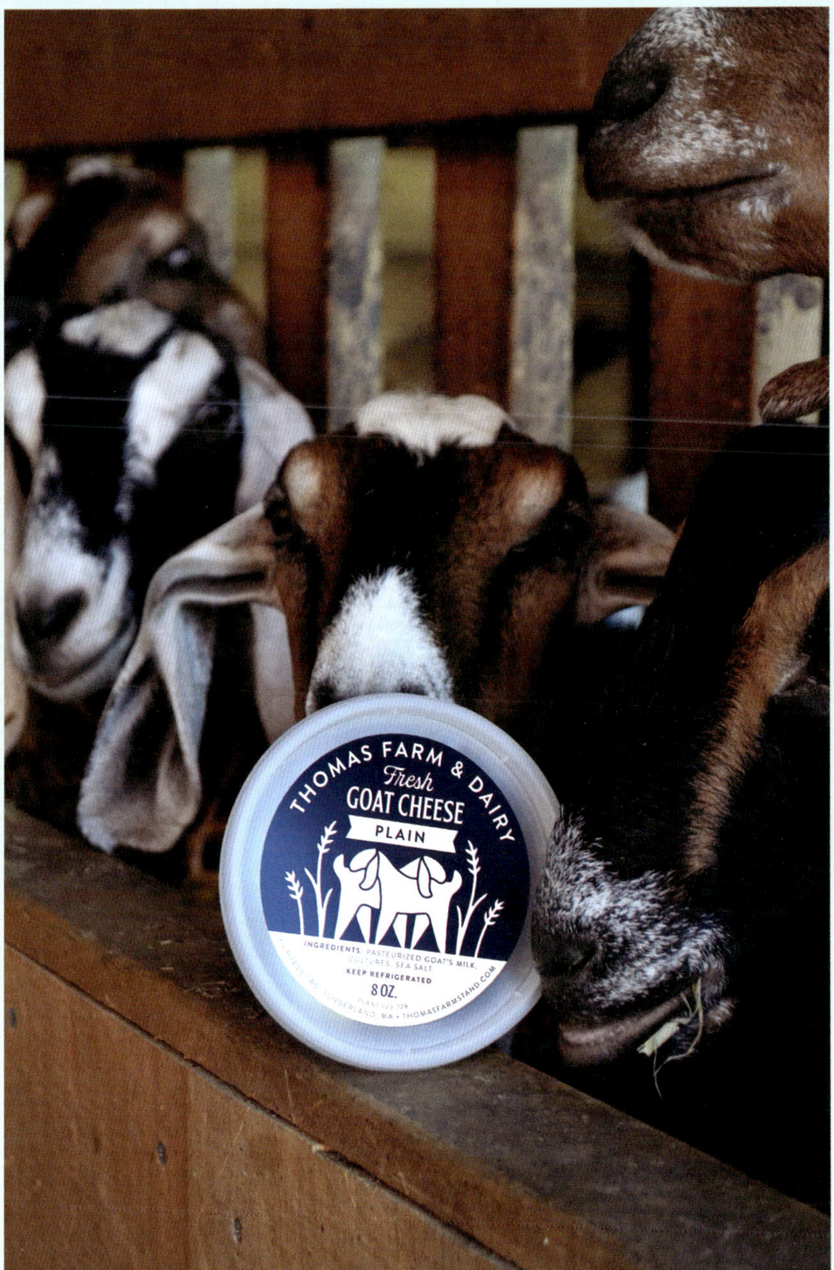

Figure 1.9 The Thomas Farm & Dairy rebrand by The Homegrown Studio included an updated label for the local farm's award-winning goat cheeses. The new look was designed to standout on grocery store shelves and help customers easily differentiate flavors. Image courtesy of The Homegrown Studio.

It was my dream one day to have my own design business, but it's hard to leave health insurance and a steady paycheck behind. It would have taken me a lot of courage to walk away myself, so the timing of that pink slip and the CISA opportunity was all pretty serendipitous. It felt devastating in the moment, but getting let go from a job I felt so safe in ended up being one of the best things that ever happened to me.

She did not start looking for another full-time job right away, and instead determined she could rely on her savings, severance package, and a few current freelance projects for three months to see if running her own design business was a viable way of supporting herself. "Creative freedom and financial freedom are closely intertwined for me. I think solid advice for anyone pursuing the goal of full-time freelance is to set a clear financial plan. That sense of security allows for deep, intentional creative exploration, which leads to regular work." Five years later, The Homegrown Studio continues to be Alessandra's main source of income.

Listening is a learned skill

Her work with CISA has continued, such as the recent project where she designed logos and other branded materials for immigrants from Puerto Rico and refugees from Somalia and Nepal, who are now farmers in Western Massachusetts. "This particular work has made me consider what my role as a designer is on a whole new level. These farmers have sacrificed so much to be here, and the value they offer our community is so great." For these projects, Alessandra worked with an interpreter, as many of the farmers did not speak English. "It really brought me back to the all-importance of listening in the design process—even though the client wasn't speaking the same language as me." Alessandra acknowledged listening was a skill she had to learn to develop in her early years of freelancing. "I learned that I needed to resist the urge to tell my clients that 'this is what I think your brand should look like', and instead actively listen to what their vision for their business was. We build our brand strategy around that. Once I made that shift towards listening intentionally, my client process and my designs became much stronger."

She also emphasized the importance of understanding your client's needs and designing practical solutions that will actually work for them. "The Puerto Rican and Somali Bantu farmers typically did not have access to computers, so design files in a Dropbox folder weren't going to be very useful to them. Instead, they needed more tangible solutions that would be helpful in running their businesses day-to-day." Alessandra collaborated with the clients to ensure they had eye-catching T-shirts featuring their new logos, premade product labels, and stamps that allowed

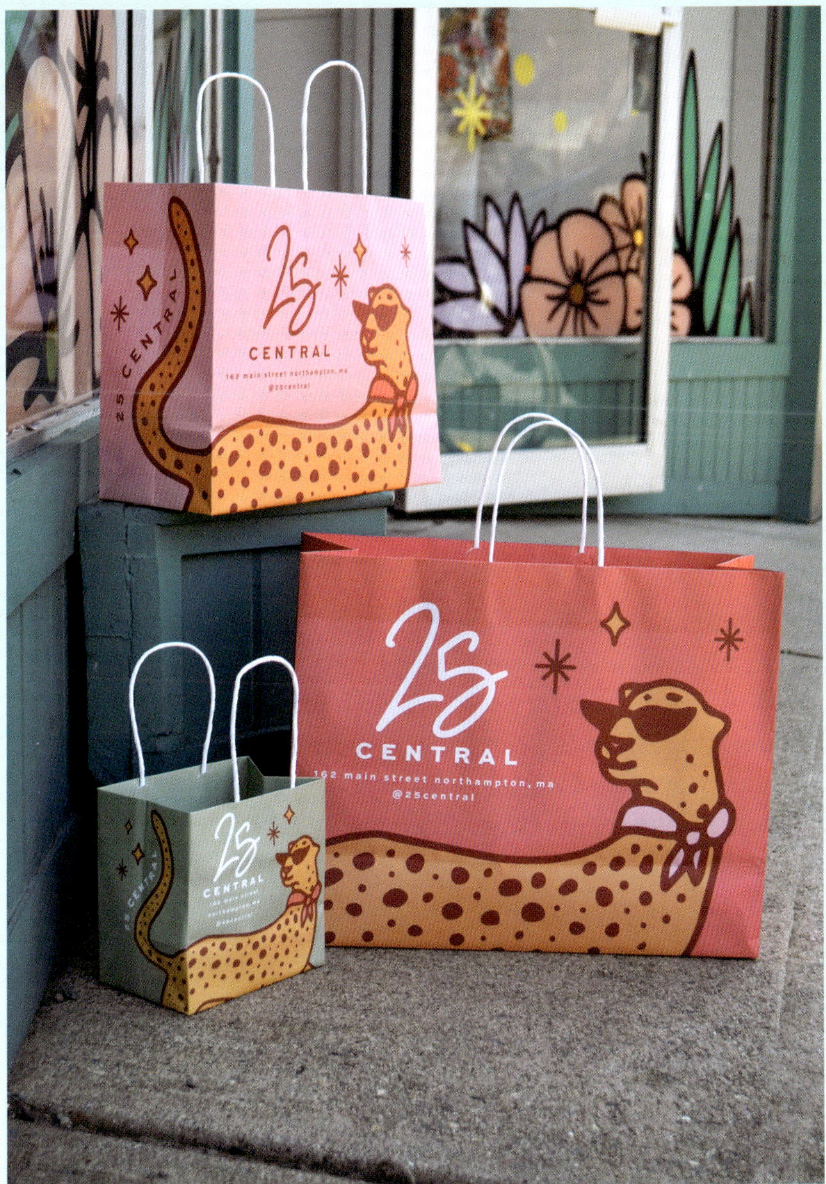

Figure 1.10 The Homegrown Studio rebranded 25 Central, a local clothing store around since the 1980s, when it made the move to a new location on Main Street in Northampton, MA, USA. The updated shopping bag designs highlight the new chic mascot, which was an homage to the iconic leopard print shopping bags from the original brand that longtime customers knew and loved. Image courtesy of The Homegrown Studio.

for "on-the-go branding" before the project concluded. It was critical the farmers had these readymade designs for the branding work to truly make an impact.

Design the community you want to be a part of

Alessandra's clientele began to expand beyond local farms through her personal network. A photographer friend she did branding work for referred her along to the owners of Familiars Coffee & Tea based in Northampton, Massachusetts. They soon hired her to rebrand the shop, then they recommended her to 25 Central, a clothing store located one street away. Alessandra describes this word-of-mouth business as "a lovely cycle of friends passing on info to friends," and she finds the only requirement for obtaining this type of work is simply to be a nice person. "It's free to be nice! I think of kindness as the least-expensive marketing initiative you can invest in for your business. If you go above and beyond for a client, and strive to make the whole experience of working together pleasant, they often can't help but tell their friends."

The branding for both Familiars and 25 Central welcome people into these businesses and make the downtown a place people want to be.

> **Northampton has seen some tougher times in recent years. I remember as a teenager I saw the city as such a lively, magical place, and I try to recreate a little bit of that feeling whenever I design a brand that will live in this town. I think glimmers of hope for a community can come in the form of thoughtful design, and I like to think the work I do can make the places we live a little brighter.**

Alessandra admires her clients' drive and how their dreams have helped bring positive change to small towns such as Northampton.

> **The success of small businesses and our communities can only be credited to the passionate people who bring incredible ideas to the table, and are excited and willing to do whatever it takes to shape their visions into reality and offer something unique to their community. That's really what keeps me motivated to put out good work and help bring those visions to life where I can.**

Freelance work is still work

The one thing Alessandra didn't expect about running her own design business is that, "This shit can be stressful! I always thought freelancing must be the most fun career you could ever have, but the fact is that it's still work, and it can be really hard." She acknowledges that it can be challenging to completely step away from work, and it can sometimes feel as though all the responsibilities of running a business are falling on your shoulders, whether it's project management or figuring out taxes. "Sure, I'm my own boss in theory, but remaining accountable and accessible to an ever-growing list of clients whose success I feel very invested in often feels like more pressure than answering to a manager ever did. It's an entirely different sense of obligation, and I don't take it lightly."

She said she avoids the term "work-life balance" because "it feels like this ideal we're expected to aspire to. I definitely take vacations and try not to work on the weekends, but I've come to accept that my work and my life are dynamically intertwined, and I'm grateful for that." Her advice to new freelancers navigating their own balance is to always stay honest with clients.

> **I wanted to promise clients the world in the beginning, but I've learned to be realistic about how much I can accomplish at a given time. It's a matter of knowing yourself, managing your time, and planning effectively, but sometimes it's also about granting yourself some grace. Last week, I was sick and I sent all my clients expecting deliverables an email that I was going to need to push deadlines back one week. Everyone understood and wished me well! Sometimes we forget the world won't end due to a missed deadline, and that as long as we are doing our best, clients tend to be very understanding. It's about clear, honest communication at the end of the day.**

She also encourages new freelancers to "flex their creativity muscle." In slow times "create prompts for yourself, make fake logos, or just doodle. In my experience, it's pretty difficult to create a stunning logo just sitting around waiting for inspiration to strike. If you've been regularly exercising your creative muscles, you've really been practicing for when that big client project comes along." She encourages sharing the content from these exercises and to not be self-conscious about putting it out there for others to see. "You'll start to develop a portfolio and a recognizable style, and that's when you'll start to stick in the minds of prospective clients."

Continuing to grow

Alessandra recently hired her good friend, Sara Esthus, who she worked with at her corporate job years before. She knew they worked well together from this experience and is enjoying having a colleague in the studio.

After working independently for several years, I feel like this more collaborative working style has unlocked a whole new side of my creativity. I love that I can send Sara concepts I'm working on, and she has instant feedback, and often pitches ideas I never even considered. I'm making better work alongside Sara, and together we're serving clients more effectively than ever. It's been very fulfilling and a lot of fun.

Alessandra and Sara are also actively partnering with other woman-led creative businesses to build what they like to call "the anti-ad agency," developing a network of trusted local resources rather than a single big agency. The women retain their small independent businesses but share client work with one another when it's appropriate. This working model allows each creative to offer an expanded menu of services to their clients, without taking on additional employees or expenses.

"It feels important to provide each other a support system at this growth stage of our individual careers. We've all been freelancing for a while now and feel comfortable with a consistent stream of clients, but we want to remain inspired and avoid overwhelm." Alessandra said some of the women will often come to her home office on Mondays and work together, which "gets us thinking more creatively and collaboratively. I've gotten many of my best ideas from the conversations we have when we're working together in-person."

To learn more about Alessandra and The Homegrown Studio:

thehomegrownstudio.com
@thehomegrownstudio

2

If someone is interested in working with you

"First date" phase

Someone is interested in working with you—congrats! You've now entered the "first date" phase of freelancing. See Figure 2.1 for an overview of a project timeline, and to learn where the "first date" phase occurs. While it may seem silly or even a little risqué to compare your client work to your romantic life, it's an apt metaphor to help make the unfamiliar—the freelancing process—seem more relatable.

Like a real first date, this phase is about learning if the other person, in this case a potential client, is a good match for you. The goal is not to get married (sign a contract) or start a family together (design something) right then and there. Instead, it's to determine if you want to pursue a more serious relationship (working together). You need to find out the basics about them—their background, their design needs, and what they're looking for in a design partner—to see if you align with one another. Like dating, sometimes you'll have great chemistry right away, and other times it will be really awkward. Listen to your gut about who you decide to pursue for client work.

You might initially "match" with many prospective clients. That can be exciting and flattering—you think, "*They want to work with me?!*" You can revel in those feel-good emotions, but do not let them cloud your judgment. Remember, how many first dates actually turn into something worthwhile? Not many, unfortunately. This is why so many romantic first dates take place in quick, cheap and easy spots such as coffee shops and pubs—no one wants to overcommit themselves, their time, or

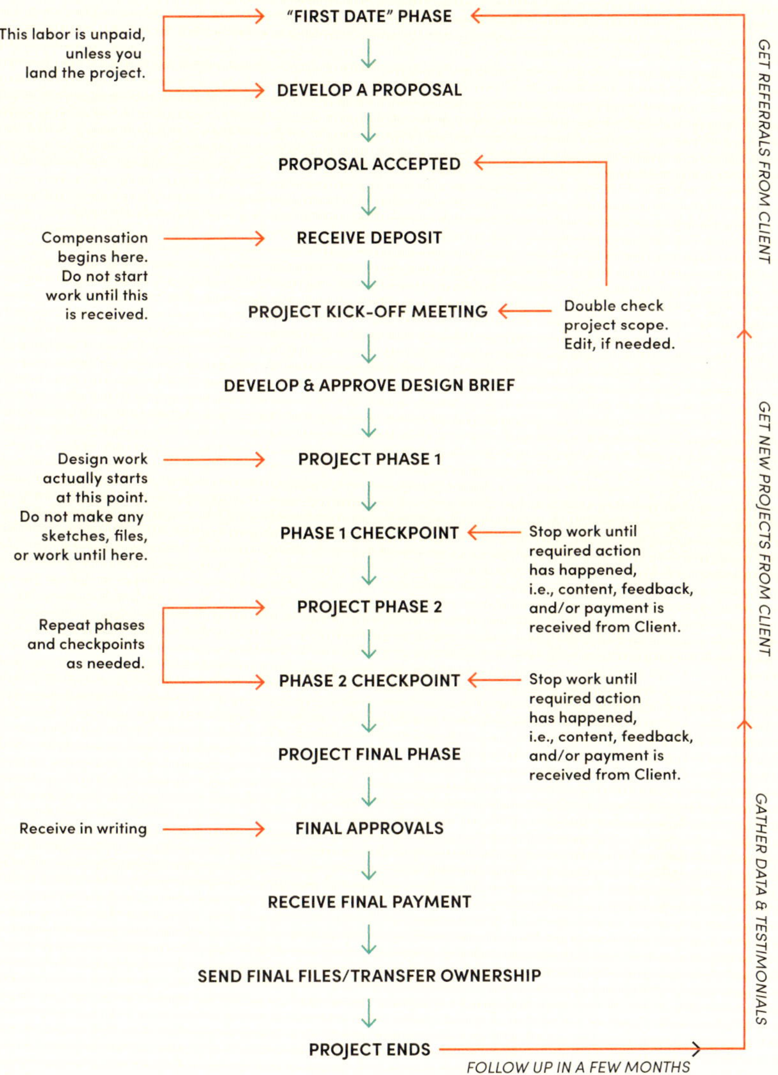

Figure 2.1 Timeline of a project.

their money at this early stage in a relationship. With potential clients, it's the same: you have to be mindful of how much you are giving to the other person without a serious commitment. There is no guarantee of a paid project after this "first date" phase. You have to quickly figure out if the potential client has promise, and if not, move on and find a better match for you.

If they seem like a client you'd like to go steady with (design for), your next step will be to create a proposal that outlines the scope of the project and how you suggest working together. You'll learn how to develop a proposal in "If you want to pursue the project," later in this chapter. To write this document, you'll use information you gathered on your "first date"; this is why it is important to ask targeted questions and take good notes in this phase.

Later in this chapter, I also give tailored advice for how to proceed with specific types of potential clients; someone you're uncomfortable charging your full rate (page 57), another designer (page 58), or someone you're not familiar with (page 60). For now, the information I've detailed below applies to any potential client, no matter who they are.

Where to have your "first dates"?

Email, phone or video calls, and in-person meet-ups are all possibilities—each method has its pros and its cons. Whatever option(s) you choose, keep in mind the "first date" phase is uncompensated labor. It's critical to get the information you need efficiently. While not every "first date" with a potential client needs to be driven by the adage "time is money," you must protect your energy and not get taken advantage of. To do this, I employ these communication channels progressively; I start with the least intensive and ramp up if things are going well with the potential client. Here's what I mean:

1. Email is often your first contact point with a potential client. To continue with the dating metaphor, email is like looking through someone's online dating profile; it gives you a sense of who they are, but it can feel impersonal. However, it is a good first screening tool to get the basic information about the *project scope—the requirements and limits of the job such as deliverables, timeline, and budget*. Email also gives you a sense of what the person might be like to work with—perhaps they offer little information, lack professionalism, or take forever to respond. (You'll practice reviewing these inquires on pages 62–3, "Red flag client exercise," Figures 2.6–2.7, later in this chapter.) If the email exchanges meet my baseline criteria for a potential project, I'll then suggest a phone or video call to more formally introduce myself and get more detailed information.
2. Phone and video calls are a great next step for promising clients because it is more personal than email, but it still does not require a huge time commitment. You can be upfront about limiting it to a short—and free—call before scheduling. I usually allocate anywhere from fifteen to thirty minutes

for these depending on the complexity of the proposed project scope and number of questions I might have. When scheduling with the person, I always send a calendar invitation, as it decreases the likelihood I'll be stood up for our appointment. And trust me, I have been ghosted by potential clients for these calls. In these situations, I'm always relieved that I did not leave my desk for the no-show.

3. Most of the time, after a call, I know whether I want to pursue the project or not. However, if I feel like meeting in-person is necessary or will help me better sell my services, I'll suggest it.
4. Meeting in-person is a personal preference. I have some freelancer friends who are very giving with their time and energy in the "first date" phase; they see it as a form of networking and a better sales tool. For me, it's a case-by-case decision because it is the most time-intensive. Where I live, I most likely have to drive to meet with someone, since I live in a city suburb, and we work remotely at Unsold Studio. This travel adds time and transportation costs, and I have to purchase something, for instance a coffee, to sit somewhere. If I lived in a walkable neighborhood with an easy meet up spot, I might be more inclined to have my "first dates" in real life. With strangers, I mostly try to avoid in-person meetings, which I'll reinforce in "Special 'first date' considerations," later in this chapter. However, if I have a relationship with the person already, like a friend or family member, or it's a prospective client I'm very eager to work with, I will likely invest in an in-person "first date."

What to bring to your "first date"?

For your initial conversations, I recommend having a list of prepared questions. They serve as a guide for the conversation, ensuring you leave the "first date" with the basic information you need. If you're nervous or get distracted, the questions are there to get you back on track. I recommend preparing the questions as a template to make note-taking easy; this way, if you decide to pursue the project ("Determining if the potential project/client is a good fit," later in this chapter), you do not need to rely on your memory.

The questions listed below will provide a good foundation to begin your "first date" list with. Even if you are very familiar with the potential client, I recommend asking all the questions. Their answers might confirm what you already know, but repetition builds confidence and puts emphasis on critical information. Most importantly, it will prevent you from making any assumptions, which can lead to problems later.

Basic client questions

You need to ask questions that give you the "big idea" about the client. These questions might be:

- *What does your business/organization offer?*
- *Who is your target audience(s)?*
- *What is the history of your business/organization?*

Project specific questions

You need to ask questions that will help you define the scope of the project and determine if you can deliver what the client is looking for. These questions might be:

- ***What are your goals with this project? How do you hope this project will impact your business/organization?*** A rookie mistake I see emerging designers make is to ask the potential client what they need designed. For example, if I ask, "What do you want me to design?" I will often hear "just a logo." While yes, I can "just make a logo," as the designer, I know that a whole brand identity system is probably what they really need. However, since the potential client said they "just need a logo," any suggestion I make to include more elements will feel like I'm trying to upsell them, which might put them off.

  Potential clients are often not designers. They might think they need a new logo to attract new customers, when in fact, the issue is their subpar website. By leading with a more open-ended question that relates to their goals, it gives you the ability to make suggestions for what you could design for them to solve their problems. If I "just made a logo," the client might later be unhappy with my services because it did not solve what they hoped it would. By asking about their goals, it helps you make sure they will leave your collaboration together satisfied and be likely to recommend you to others.

  Some clients might have specific and accurate deliverable lists for their projects, but I guarantee they will be forthcoming about that when asked this question. For example, I designed promotional banners for a local museum for their seasonal exhibitions. The museum team consistently has these banners replaced throughout the year, so they are confident in their needs; they were quick to report required dimensions, materials, and content for the banners in our initial meeting.
- ***What is your timeline? Is it flexible?*** An answer you'll often hear is, "As soon as possible." Many potential clients, not knowing how the design process works, engage designers too close to their project deadline. While you cannot rewind the clock and have them reach out to you sooner, you can see if their timeline is negotiable.
- ***What is your budget?*** As you likely know, most people do not like talking about money and will avoid answering this question. Often the reason is not malicious (they are not withholding to get the best deal), but it is because the potential client simply has no idea what design costs.

  It is helpful to emphasize that by being transparent about how much they'd like to spend on the project, you can better serve them. To aid this discussion, I sometimes use a metaphor related to car shopping. I'll say something like,

  > *A project can be designed at a lower price point, but it will be like buying a clunky used car; it will work to get you from point A to point B, meeting your basic needs, but that's about it. However, if you have a bigger budget, it will be like purchasing a new luxury car; it will get you*

from point A to point B, but in style with all the latest features. If I have a better sense of your budget, I can help you 'shop the right car' for your project.

If they REALLY don't want to talk about a budget, I recommend the "bottom line test." Throw out a number you think is around the price point you anticipate (there is more about pricing in "How to price your work," in Chapter 3) and say something to the effect of, "I'm not taking on projects for less than $1,000 dollars right now. Does this work with your budget?" What I like about this "bottom-line test" is that it forces the potential client to reveal something about their budget. That number will either work for them, or it will not. If they can't afford your baseline project price, they will tell you. This saves you from doing the hard work of writing a proposal and then finding out their budget was closer to $100, which is too little an amount for you to consider the work. The "bottom-line test" also does not commit you to a project price; it is communicating the *least* amount you are charging in that moment.

If the prospective client *only* wants to talk about money, that makes me worry. If they are simply seeking out the lowest bidder for their design project, it signals to me they do not truly value my expertise as a designer. Instead, they are looking for someone to be their "computer mouse-clicker" rather than a collaborator.

- ***Who is the project decision-maker(s)?*** It is good to know if you will be managing the expectations of one person, or two people, or a board of ten people.

For your information

- ***Have you worked with a designer before?*** If the potential client says, "Yes, I've worked with a designer before," this allows you to ask questions such as "What did you like/dislike from that experience with that designer?" That kind of information is extremely valuable. For example, a potential client once told us they did not like that their previous designer would "disappear into their studio." That told us that the potential client wanted to be engaged and feel involved throughout the design process—which is good to know ahead of time.

  If the potential client says, "No, they haven't worked with a designer before" this means you'll need to be a guide for them throughout the process. You also might need to educate them about the value of design.
- ***What design tools do you have access to and/or use?*** A common complaint I've heard from many clients is that while a designer has created something great for them, the files they hand-off are hard for the client to implement on their own. While you're the design expert and use industry programs and tools, most of your clients will not have access or know how to use them. For many small-scale clients like you'll begin working with, they do not have the budget to hire a designer for every design-related task they have. Often a designer is brought in to help get them started in the right direction

and leave them with tools, so they can do-it-themselves after that. This is why it is helpful to know what capabilities your potential client has, and to know how you might need to create certain deliverables to meet their day-to-day needs.

- ***How do you like to communicate and work with others?*** One of the biggest components to running a successful freelance project is good communication. You can directly ask how they prefer to communicate, such as email, phone, video conferencing, or in-person meetings. Learning if they prefer to have monthly, weekly, or daily meetings will indicate their demand on your time (and also your price point). For example, designer Aaliyah Moore (interview, page 143) says:

  > *I learned to ask about the client's response time for emails after working with someone who was slower to respond than I accounted for in my proposed timeline. When I worked with that client, the whole schedule that I proposed became quickly inaccurate because I assumed a faster response time, say two days, rather than the week it actually took them to get back to me. Now to create more realistic timelines for proposals* [see "Creating a realistic timeline," in Chapter 3, for more information], *I ask up front about how long they normally take to review emails, which helps me to decide how many days—or weeks—to plan for them to review designs and provide me with feedback.*

- ***How did they hear about me?*** It's good to know if your business comes from word-of-mouth (thank the person who referred you), your social media (keep posting!), an internet search (thank you, SEO words), or other means so you can continue to market yourself effectively in those arenas.
- ***Is there anything you think is important for me to know about the project that we did not discuss? Do you have any questions for me?*** I always like to end the "first date" with these types of questions. They indicate the conversation is wrapping up, but also gives the potential client an opportunity to add and reinforce important information. If the potential client has any concerns, this also gives you a chance to alleviate them.

What to not bring to your "first date"?

Sketches or design solutions

In the "first date" phase, you are not being paid for your services yet. This means you are not designing anything yet. That comes once you've made a serious commitment to one another (see Chapter 4, "Working together," for more information).

You have to protect your biggest asset—your ideas. If you offer a sketch or something before officially agreeing to work together (after the proposal is signed and a project deposit has been received), there's nothing stopping that person from taking your idea to another designer or using a free design tool themselves to implement it.

If someone tries to pressure you to design something for them, give them design feedback or give your ideas away for free at this stage, redirect them to your portfolio. Point to an example of something you've made before that demonstrates a similar or related solution. You can also politely say, "We'll tackle that once we've officially begun the design process together. At that point, I'll have had more time with your project to give my best recommendations."

A negative attitude

People want to work with folks that give them "good vibes" and you have to show up to these "first dates" as the best version of yourself. Even if you do not end up working with the potential client in that moment, they might become one later or recommend you to someone else.

Matey (interview, page 50) said they've picked up work from "failed" prospective clients: "We've gotten jobs from people who initially reached out to us for design work, but we never actually worked together for whatever reason. Even though a project did not happen with them, they've gone on to recommend us for other opportunities that we've landed."

If you've completed your "first date," move ahead to "Determining if the potential project/client is a good fit," later in this chapter.

Interview

Matey

Shelton and Josh Carnley are the founders of Matey (formerly known as Studio Carnley), a branding team located in Birmingham, Alabama, a place that is not often identified as a design hub. However, their talent is changing that perception about the city. Since opening in 2019, their work has garnered recognition from The Dieline, Brand New, and Delish.com. By choosing to root the studio in their home state, Matey is defining what Southern design is today.

Matey's love and pride for the American South oozes from their work. Their portfolio is filled with businesses that celebrate the heritage of the region, such as North Carolina-based Highlands Smokehouse, "a roadside barbeque staple," Alabama-based Mentone Market, a general store "perched atop Lookout Mountain for 80 years and counting," and Golden Eagle syrup that "has been used on pecan pies and on biscuits by hungry Southerners for generations." Their designs nod to the visual history of the South, while adding a fresh contemporary spin.

The duo's working relationship began in an unlikely way: as cheerleaders at Auburn University (Auburn, Alabama). Trust was built between them as Shelton flew high in the air, and Josh was there as the base to catch her. Now married with three children, the couple's energetic spirit, self-discipline, and risk-taking from their cheerleading days has carried over into the success of Matey. Now they rally around their clients, using design to uplift their community, from mom-and-pop shops to dollar-store sweet treats and college town bars. Let Matey's positivity rub off on you and motivate you to take the next leap in your freelancing journey.

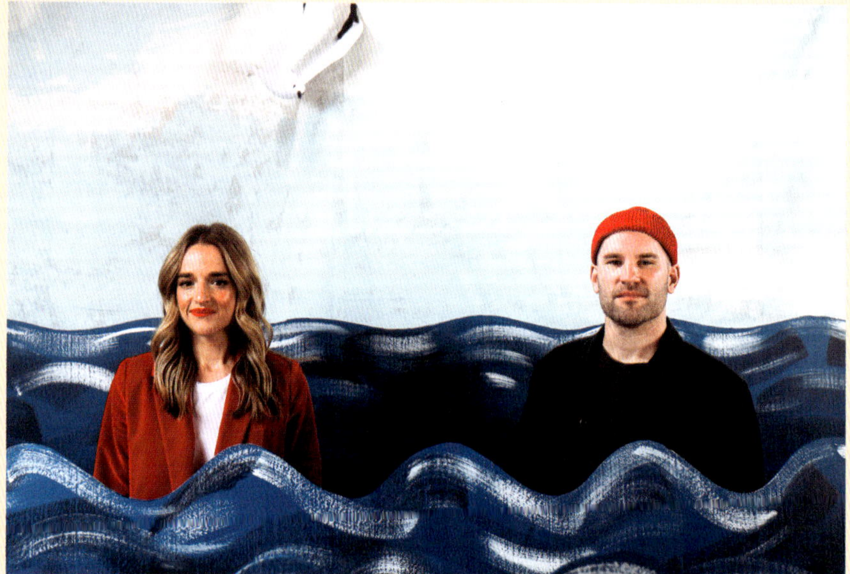

Figure 2.2 Portrait of Matey, Josh and Shelton Carnley.

You have to be brave (and a little naïve)

"I can't explain it, but I truly saw something special in him," Shelton says about meeting Josh on the cheer team, where it was uncommon for art and design students like him to belong. "Designers can have an ego about them where they're cool, silky, and everything cheerleading is not, but Josh wasn't like that. He's always stepped outside of his comfort zone." By following his diverse interests and being unafraid to join various communities around campus, Josh learned how to work with a wide array of people. As a student, he leveraged his different networks to begin taking on select "very, very local" freelance projects. Josh recommends expanding your circle beyond fellow creatives: "Most of your clients will lack a design vocabulary, so you have to practice communicating with people who don't know anything about design."

Upon graduation, Josh and Shelton moved away from Alabama, pursuing careers in other states. Shelton says she didn't feel passionate about nutrition, which she'd received her degree in, and began working in ad sales. Meanwhile, Josh was hired on the design side of an agency but continued to take on freelancing projects outside of his full-time role. The couple maintain these types of positions in the studio today; Shelton is the Business Development Director, while Josh is the Creative Director.

A few years into their careers, the Carnleys were comfortable; they'd settled in Atlanta, Georgia with "great, flexible jobs" and welcomed their first child together. When their daughter was about a year old, Josh began making more money from his freelancing design work than from his agency salary: an ongoing freelance client offered him a well-paid six-month retainer project. "Even though it felt like a no brainer for Josh to quit his job and pursue the freelancing work, all of the odds were against us. We had so much pressure and responsibility, especially with our daughter."

However, they decided to follow their instinct and pursed opening their own studio. "We worked in the design industry long enough to know there's no such thing as a stable job—you can always get fired. We knew that if we crashed and burned running our own business, we could always go back working somewhere and get insurance."

Josh laughingly says, "You kind of have to have a lapse in judgment. We did back then, and it really helped because it made a freelance career seem doable. Now we have three kids and both of our incomes are dependent on the studio, we look back and we're like, 'How the hell did this even happen?'"

However, both agree working for themselves was the right decision for them. Shelton acknowledges that the Carnleys are natural risktakers:

People are going to tell you that you need to think logically and make sure your ducks are in a row before starting, but we are not those people. When someone says they might want to have a third kid, we're like just do it. Or they say they want to buy a new house, we're like just do it. It's in our personalities to just go for it.

Josh adds, "You can prep all you want, but you just have to go for it. You can learn the business stuff along the way."

To the moon

Shelton and Josh were committed to making Matey a success. "We knew for the first three years we were going to take on every single project that came our way. We worked a lot, and we're still working a lot, but in the early days we had to take on a bunch of jobs to prove to ourselves that we could do this." They note, "The great thing about being a graphic designer is that even though jumping out on your own is super scary, you can always find a gig. It may be working for your cousin's friend's uncle's boss, and it might not be glamorous, but there's always work to be had." It's important to remember not every project needs to be portfolio worthy. Shelton and Josh have done projects that "paid the bills, but we would never show anyone because it's not the type of work we want to attract."

To draw in the types of clients they wanted to work with, Josh and Shelton began casually reaching out to people in businesses they admired. For instance, they connected with the owner of Plaza, a bar and lounge located in their former college town. In their introduction, they complimented the business, lightly pitched Matey's design services, and said something to the effect of, "We're not sure what you're planning for the future, but as you grow or add more restaurants, we're around." Their strategy to build casual acquaintances with these types of folks worked. Eventually, the Plaza owner reached out to them with a project; they had bounced around with a few different design studios but hadn't found the right fit. They asked if Josh and Shelton would be interested in the job, one with a tight timeline (six weeks over the Christmas holidays) and a modest budget—Matey accepted.

One of the deliverables for the brief included exterior signage to attract patrons. Shelton described how Plaza is located in a neighborhood that is a little fancy, so they agreed the sign needed to be clean to match the area, but because it is a pub-style restaurant they had to "dirty it up a little." This is one of the strengths of Matey's work; the ability to seamlessly balance highbrow and lowbrow aesthetics. To do this, their idea was to have an old vacuum form sign, "not just something printed politely on a little hanger." The sign-style was chosen because "we want the sign to get a little moldy, a little yellowy, a little worn over time, and we knew it would do that."

To execute their vision, Josh and Shelton found a sign maker, but there was a caveat: the vendor could not deliver, and they were located four hours away. Undeterred, the duo made the long drive themselves, loaded the sign in their car, and hired a local electrician to hang and wire it at Plaza. They'd gone above and beyond because of their dedication to their vision, and their client. Josh says about moments like this, "You have to create the things you want to be a part of, like we want to have a drink at Plaza when we're visiting Auburn."

These types of slow-burn network connections have paid off time and again for Matey. Back when Shelton was still working in ad sales, she pursued Moon Pie,

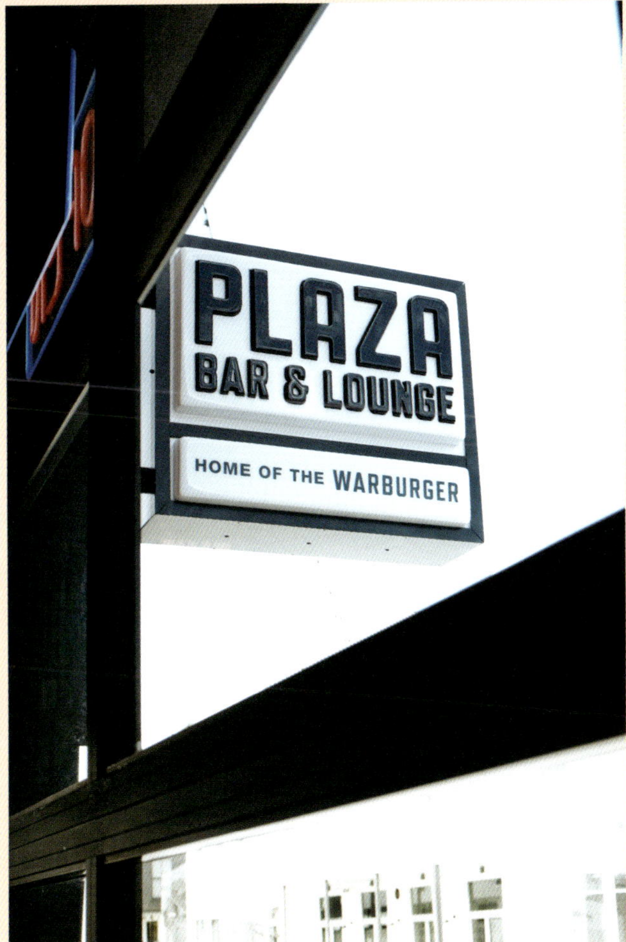

Figure 2.3 A vacuum-form sign was designed and produced for Plaza, a high-brow dive bar located in Auburn, Alabama, as part of Matey's branding package for the client.

a 100- year-old baked treat company well known in the southern United States, to purchase ad space in a magazine. After receiving her inquiry, the Moon Pie owner checked out Shelton's LinkedIn profile. There he realized that his son-in-law cheered with Josh and Shelton when they were at Auburn University. "We had no clue our good friend was married to this guy's daughter." Because of this, the Moon Pie owner replied to Shelton about her sales request.

Through the years, Shelton continued to chat with him on and off, "building up a rapport and a friendship even before he decided to work with us." When Matey launched, she made sure he knew about it, even though Moon Pie already had a design agency they contracted with. Months later, the owner asked if they would design Moon Pie's holiday tins. He was unhappy with the concepts their usual agency had pitched, so Moon Pie decided to give Shelton and Josh a chance. Again, they were given a tight timeline for a highly desirable client: "We found out on like December 20th and it was due January 7th." They made it work, and that quick turnaround project paid off. Matey continues to create the Fall and Winter tins for Moon Pie, and also expanded their reach with the company by pitching an idea for Valentine's Day boxes, an untapped market. Josh and Shelton's business savvy made a new revenue stream for Moon Pie: the first-time limited edition Valentine's Day boxes now sell out within days after their release.

The Carnleys' ability to network and build meaningful relationships has proven to be an asset, but occasionally it poses challenges. "We treat our clients as if they're family. Sometimes because they feel so comfortable with us, they call us with a need and expect us to turnaround design work for them immediately. We try to accommodate them, but that type of piecemeal work can interrupt our planned to-do list." However, Josh says it's important to remain friendly in these moments because a time might come when you need a second chance. "We've had to apologize to our clients before because we've messed up. Because our relationships extend to friendships with many of our clients, it has given us a lot of grace. Shelton has a principle of never burning a bridge that we try to implement."

The couple focuses on the positive when adversity arises at Matey: "You have to have an optimistic view of your clients and projects. Sometimes the bright side is that the project gives you financial stability, or your work is giving your client the flexibility to be with their family more. Those things have to be good enough."

Be proud of your town

Matey's brand identities for Birmingham establishments such as June Coffee, film and photo studio Good Sport, and a local tiki bar create local charm for the Alabama city. Shelton says, "I hope with our work we're saving Birmingham from just becoming and looking like anywhere else."

By working with clients in the place where their office and home are located, the Carnleys often see the firsthand reaction to their design work.

Shelton told a story about when she was a kid, her architect father would point out all the projects he'd worked on when they'd drive through their town. Now,

The great reason to work within your community is you get to see the response. You get to see people supporting the stuff you're a part of, like murmuring about the cool menus or taking photos in front of the sign you designed. They're excited that the place exists. These folks are proud of what you've done, even if they don't know you made that work.

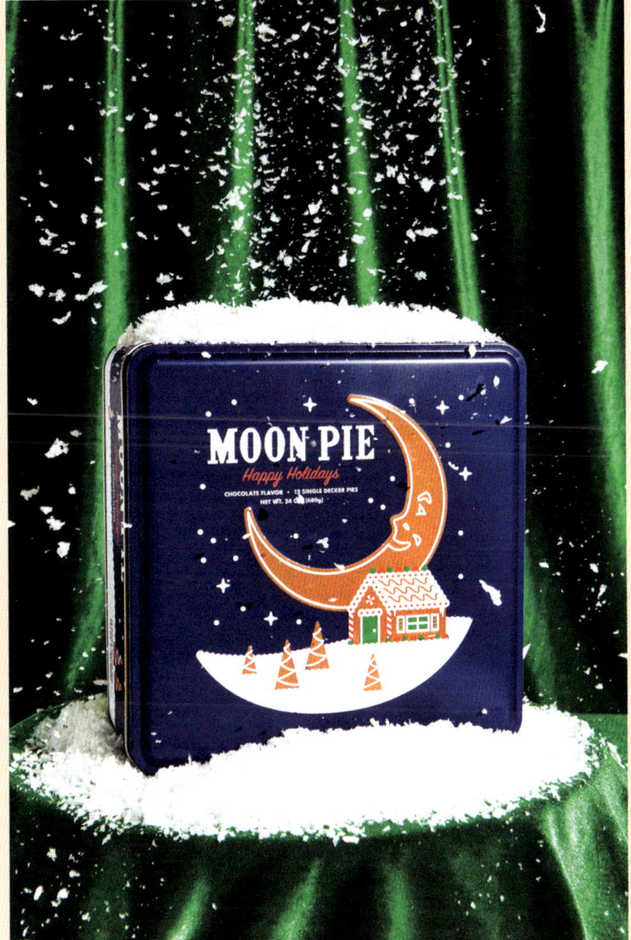

Figure 2.4 A limited edition seasonal tin designed for Moon Pie, a sweet treat company that's been in business for over 100 years.

her and Josh have that type of experience with their own children at local spots such as June. "We take our kids there all the time, and the coffee bags are at eye level for them. Our oldest daughter will look at us and say, 'You did all the drawings for this right?' The fact that you can be prideful to your family, whether you have kids or not, is pretty cool."

Their commitment to Alabama continues to grow. Josh says, "Our first two years in business, we probably had 15 percent of our clients be Alabama-based. Then the third year it grew to 25 or 30 percent. This last year, 50 percent of our clients are from Alabama." Shelton adds, "I want to sink my teeth in Alabama. When someone opens a business in the state, I want to be the first people they think of to hire for design."

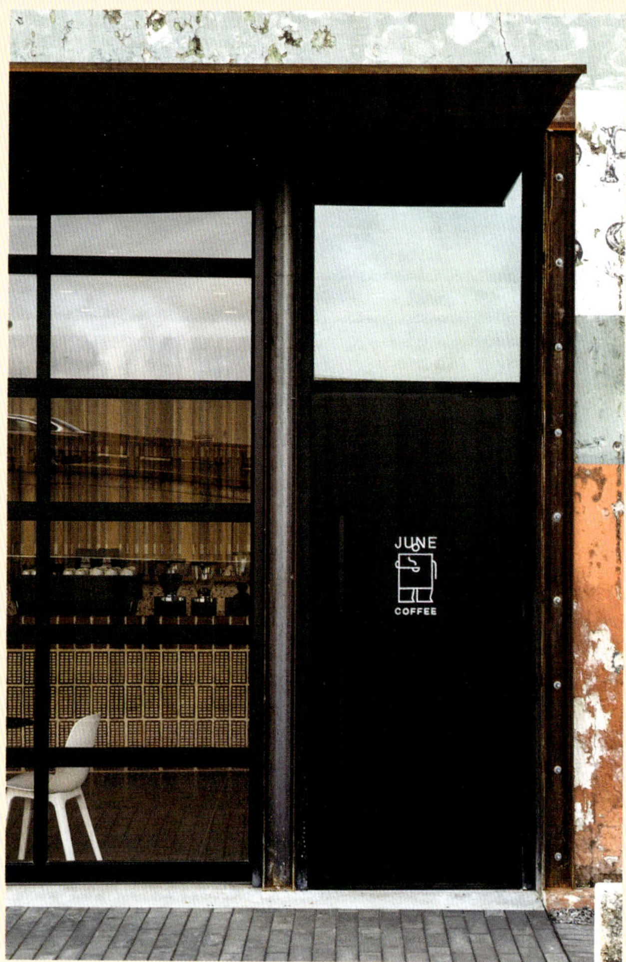

Figure 2.5 Matey's rebrand for June, a coffee shop and roasting company in Birmingham, Alabama that aimed to create cohesion between architecture, place, and brand.

To learn more about Josh, Shelton, and Matey:

weart matey.com
@wearematey

Special "first date" considerations

Some types of people require additional considerations before you decide to pursue freelance work with them. If you have not yet read "'First date' phase," at the start of this chapter, I recommend going back there to get the basics down first.

People you feel uncomfortable charging your full rate

This section gives advice for situations where you feel uncomfortable charging your normal rate, such as for pro bono projects or when the client is also your bestie.

I guarantee, whether you want them to or not, a person you know will have a design project for you. One of my early freelance gigs was for a local restaurant in my hometown where I waitressed in the summers. The owners knew I went to school for design, so when they needed to update their menus, they asked if I could help. And to make matters worse, they wanted to pay me—just kidding, well, sort of. Talking about money with strangers is hard enough, but charging your boss, even weirder.

Relationships with those closest to us often are the trickiest. Add business to the mix, it can get messy fast. No relationship is worth ruining over a design project, so I recommend a couple of ways to keep your most important relationships in-tact while delivering design services.

1. ***Set boundaries by treating them like a "real" full-paying client.*** This might feel icky, but it is in everyone's best interest. They should respect you for protecting your relationship by establishing some ground rules around the design project.

   You need to go through the "first date" phase with this person, but perhaps you skip right to meeting in-person if you know them well. You still need to ask your templated questions, *all of them.* If you decide to design for them, you need to create a proposal (see Chapter 3, "If you want to pursue the project"), even a "lite version," to make everyone agrees on what's expected.

   One of our early clients for Unsold Studio was a friend. They were starting a business, we were starting a business, it made sense to help one another out. We verbally agreed that we would create a brand for them, and once they got on their feet, they would pay us. Sounds okay, right? But how do you measure "getting on their feet"? For almost a year, we did continuous free work for them without any talk of payment. Resentment was beginning to grow, but it boiled over when our friend took a vacation to a tropical location. Surely if they could afford an all-inclusive resort, they could begin to pay us something for our services? We had to have an uncomfortable conversation with our friend soon after to resolve the issue. If we'd made a more formal agreement, such as outlining that we would create ten hours of free work per month for up to six months, or something like that, from the beginning, we could have avoided the situation altogether.

By treating these folks like any other client, it helps them to see you as a professional. Another early project I took on was designing a logo for my dad's new business (thanks, JB!). It would have been easy to fall into our father/daughter relationship, where he is typically the leader. By setting expectations as if he was any other client, this balanced our normal power dynamic; it allowed him to see me as a design expert and a collaborator during the project.

2. ***Give them a deal but show them the market rate.*** When you develop a proposal for their project, you must show the *"market rate"—the standard price for services*—alongside the deal you decide to give them. This helps the recipient understand the value of your work and gives them perspective on the deal that they're getting. This establishes the value of design, which is helpful to any future designers that they might hire. For instance, imagine that you've been charging your cousin $25/hour without communicating that it's a discounted rate. A time comes when you're unable to do the work for them, so you refer your cousin to your designer friend. Your designer friend proposes to charge them $75/hour—the market rate—and your cousin balks at the price. They can't believe that it costs that much, and they haggle with your designer friend to come down in price. In your cousin's mind, design shouldn't be that expensive because they haven't paid that much before. If they had known the market rate, this higher price point would not come as such a shock and the situation could have been avoided.

   Those closest to us can be our best advocates. If you do a great job for them, I bet they will be the first to tell their networks to hire you. By showing them the market rate in your proposal (e.g., $75/hour), it also helps prevent them from promoting your services at the discounted rate because they know your market rate.

   But what is the discount you should offer, you ask? You could have a tiered system—family get a 50 percent discount, friends 25 percent, and friends of friends 10 percent. You could also agree on a trade. When I was a design student, there was a rumor one of my design professors exchanged a brand identity system for a year's worth of beer from their brewery client. Free is also an option if that feels better to your moral compass. Whatever you decide is your deal, you have to outline it clearly, as well as the market value in your proposal.

Other designers

This section outlines considerations that are specific to working with another designer, whether they hire you themselves or pass along design projects to you.

If they want to hire you to design a project for them

As mentioned, sometimes designers will hire a freelancer to help them on a project-by-project basis. You are not their full-time employee. Instead, you might be referred to as a "subcontractor" or an "independent contractor."

If you are working for a more established designer, they often will take the lead in this scenario—let them and learn from them. After the "first date" phase, they might present you with a proposal to sign. Like a client proposal (learn more in Chapter 3, "If you want to pursue the project"), their version should similarly outline things such as the deliverables, timeline, payment schedule, and other details about working together. If presented to you, it is important you understand all the terms and conditions before agreeing to the job. If something is not clear to you, ask the designer for clarification. Below, I've listed two questions I've found emerging designers do not always know to ask:

1. ***Will you retain promotional rights to the design work you produce?*** Are you allowed to feature any of the project in your personal portfolio? If so, be sure to properly credit your role on the job. If you cannot share this work publicly, you might consider asking for a slightly higher rate as you will not benefit by promoting the work and garnering new projects from it.
2. ***Is there a "non-compete clause"?*** Some contracts will outline that you cannot work for any of the designer's competitors. They might also state you cannot design for any of their client's competitors, for instance, if you're being sub-contracted to design for dog treat company A, can you freelance independently for dog treat company B? And what if dog treat company A directly approaches you to take on a future project? While this might not feel ethical to accept—could you?

If the other designer does not present you with some kind of agreement, do not be afraid to present them with your own proposal (head to Chapter 3, "If you want to pursue the project," if needed). This might feel uncomfortable, but it's important to advocate yourself. To reiterate, the other designer should welcome this from you, especially since it protects both your interests. And if they're not keen on the idea, they might not be the best person to freelance for after all.

If they pass along potential design work to you

Send a thank you note

Make sure to acknowledge a designer's recommendation of you, especially if you'd like to continue receiving project leads from them. At Unsold Studio, we once met an emerging designer who was eager for work. In the span of a few weeks, we connected them to multiple clients with small jobs that we were unable to take on.

A few months later, the designer shared project images on their social media from one of the clients we referred to them. It felt great that we'd successfully directed the client to another designer and had helped the emerging designer land some business. However, the emerging designer never sent us any acknowledgment or expressed any gratitude for these leads. After that, we removed them from our list of designers we recommend.

While this might seem petty, we felt a bit used. We also worried that if we continued to recommend them, would they similarly snub a client? When you refer someone, you're endorsing them. You're saying that you're confident in their abilities, both design and professional. By being dismissive of us, we lost this confidence in them, and they lost us as a resource for potential projects. A simple "thank you," even if the recommendation does not work out for you, goes a long way. Designer Naoma Serna-Zahn from Nuevo Studio (interview, page 132) said, "A thank you does not have to be sent in the mail; email is perfectly fine. Although, a thank you note in the mail is way better."

Ask for information, if you feel comfortable

It's totally okay to follow up with the designer to ask questions about the client. Are they passing off a client they've worked with before? If so, do they have any tips for working with them effectively? Fellow designers will usually be forthcoming with that information if they have it.

Pay it forward

As you begin to receive more project inquiries than you can take on, share them with other designers, especially if you believe in good karma.

People you're not familiar with

This section outlines considerations that are specific to working with folks you are not familiar with.

There will come a time when your inbox lights up with a stranger's email inquiring about a project. It will be exciting, and you'll feel like you've made it. Celebrate the win, then move back into a more practical mindset.

- ***They're likely shopping around for a designer.*** You might not be the only person they are considering for their project. Remember, this is the "first date" phase—you aren't in a serious relationship yet, and there are lots of designers in the sea. My best advice is to try to not worry about who else they might be thinking of hiring. Stay in your lane—be confident about what you offer, your pricing, your timelines, your process—and know if it's meant to be, it will be.
- ***Be cautiously optimistic.*** As strangers, you and the potential client lack trust with and loyalty to one another—those are qualities that are built over time. Without an established relationship, your obligation to each other is limited. The potential client might lack empathy for the uncompensated time, labor, and energy required from you in the "first date" phase. For instance, when Unsold Studio first started, Lilian and I were so excited that anyone wanted to work with us. We'd schedule a meeting for coffee where we'd drive to the shop, arrive early (because we're anxious about parking), order drinks for us and the potential client, have a great conversation, then after an hour and a half find out they have no budget for the project. *Whomp, whomp.* We'd then

leave a little depressed that the project wasn't going to work out, but also poorer (we paid for gas, parking, and coffee) and busier (we'd spent three hours that we could have been tackling other things on our to-do lists). It was hard for us to believe the potential client would let us go through all that trouble knowing they had no way to truly pursue the project. This is why I stress the importance of honing the "first date" phase and asking the right questions early on, and why I've become guarded about in-person meetings unless I'm feeling confident about the client's or project's potential.

While I'm painting a pessimistic picture, my point is you must exercise caution and set boundaries, especially with strangers. However, there will be amazing potential clients that start as strangers and later become clients, and possibly friends.

- ***Look for "red flags."*** If you find a red flag in a potential client, this does not have to be a dealbreaker. Instead, it might indicate how you will need to work with them, if you choose to. Over time, your freelancer intuition will enhance and help guide you in spotting possible troublesome clients. Use Figures 2.6 and 2.7 to practice identifying and working with common red flags.

Determining if the potential project/client is a good fit

When I first started freelancing, I felt like I should take on every project that came my way, without questioning if it was the right fit for me *and* the potential client. Instead, my priority was feeling the high of landing a project, *any* project. After that, sometimes the project itself was less-than-stellar; I'd agreed to project scopes that were too large, outside my expertise, with too tight timelines and too small budgets. It was like an act of self-sabotage where I was setting myself and the client up for failure. Luckily, I somehow managed to deliver something to these clients and not ruin my reputation in the interim. With hindsight, my best advice is to feel like you can say no. Designer Ryan Tan from OuterEdit (interview, page 107) agreed: "Be honest about your setup, what you're capable of, and what you're comfortable doing. Honesty goes a long way running a creative company."

Not every project inquiry is going to be for you, and that's okay! Remember, this is like dating—do you expect every date to have a fairy-tale ending? Of course not! Over time, you'll begin to refine your practice and build confidence, and saying "no" will become easier.

Questions to ask yourself

Do I understand the client's project goals?

If you feel like you do not have a firm grasp on the project scope, do not be afraid to ask to connect with them again. It's better to overcommunicate and get the information correct, before proceeding to write a proposal that is inaccurate. If you're worried about annoying the potential client with follow-up questions, keep in mind it

RED FLAG CLIENT EXERCISE

NOTES:

LOOKING FOR DESIGN PARTNER

potentialclient@email.com **11:11am** (11 minutes ago)
to me

Hey!

My friends and I are looking for a new logo for our new tennis apparel company and we love your work! We are currently waiting for our investors to come through to produce the clothing line, but we need a logo as soon as possible to create mock-ups to finalize our pitch to them.

We have a logo now that a friend of a friend made. It works, but we're interested in seeing if we can make the brand look refined, but a little more cool and hip. We've attached the current logo here. Any thoughts on how we could update it to make it hit the mark? We're looking forward to hearing your thoughts!

What do you charge for logo designs? And how much time will you need to create one? As mentioned, we're under a tight deadline and are hoping to have this turned around in four weeks (or less if possible!).

Let us know what the next steps are!

Best,
Martha

YOU RECEIVE THIS AS AN EMAIL FROM A POTENTIAL CLIENT
Highlight, circle, or underline any "red flags" you see. For each "red flag" you identify, decide if it's:

- **a workable "red flag."** If so, what would you do to help manage the potential issue(s)?
- **a deal breaker.** If so, why?

Then flip to see how I'd respond to this inquiry.

Figure 2.6 Red flag client exercise, page 1.

"RED FLAGS" I SEE

MULTIPLE DECISION-MAKERS

If we work together, I'd make sure to identify one of them as the primary contact person for project management. I'd also require all the team members to be at important project milestones like the kick-off meeting and the design presentations.

"JUST A LOGO"

They mention a logo, but then a "brand" later in the email. I would kindly educate them about the difference between brand identity systems and standalone logos. I'd mention how a whole system would benefit the brand because we'd explore things like messaging, graphics for apparel, price tags, ads, social media, and other deliverables.

MONEY-FOCUSED AND IN A RUSH

I'd reply that I do not do one-off logo designs, but if they're interested in learning more about a full brand package, they start at $X amount, and normally take X amount of time. I'd emphasize that the turnaround time for the project is also dependent on the client's availability. If they want to rush the project, I could do so for an additional fee.

"WAITING FOR INVESTORS"

I'd ask what their budget is for this specific project. If they do not have money for these preliminary pieces, like "the logo," I'd tell them to reach out again once funding came in. If you want to take a financial risk, you could ask for equity in their business or another kind of trade, but that's a BIG RISK if it doesn't pan out for their company!

ASKING FOR FREE ADVICE

I'd respond that through my full design process, we'd find a solution that meets their goals. I'd redirect by asking how tied they are to the current logo's look and feel? Since their friend made it, they might be more resistant to make necessary changes. I'd want to know if I took the project on, I could fully execute a new idea.

FINAL VERDICT

I love tennis, so I'd be eager to have this client if I can make it work with them. I think most of these "red flags" are workable if the potential client seems amenable to the boundaries I'm setting:

- hiring for brand system, not a logo
- has a budget for the project
- has flexibility on the timeline, or is willing to pay a rush fee

If so, my next step would be to hop on a call with them to gather some more details. If all continues to look good, I'd develop a proposal with policies like having a primary contact person from their team.

Figure 2.7 Red flag client exercise, page 2.

shows you're detail-oriented and concerned about understanding their needs—that doesn't sound like a bad thing to me.

Do you have the ability to deliver a great product to the client?

If not, it might be wise to turn down the opportunity. If you deliver a bad experience to the client, you are risking your reputation. Word-of-mouth business from your clients is the best pipeline for future work, and if the client does not leave happy, forget about gaining access to their networks.

However, there can be exceptions to this. Sometimes design opportunities come along that we do not feel like we're ready for, but we want to take on for various reasons. For example, perhaps someone approaches you to do a motion design project. You've been wanting to add more of those types of projects to your portfolio, but are still new and are not efficient at that type of work yet. Instead of taking the project on—trying to learn on the job, rushing, making mistakes, and losing profitability on fixing things—you could be upfront with the client. You could be transparent, and say, "I do not have a lot of experience in motion design, but I've been eager to try. If you're willing to be patient with me and be my first test-case, I'll give you a discount on the project. If not, I completely understand and would be happy to recommend you to someone else."

Is the client and/or project the right fit for me, right now?

Having the right skillset to complete the project should not be the sole consideration for taking on a project. You also have to consider what your life, goals, and workload look like in that moment. For example, perhaps there's an opportunity for a project, but the budget is small. Normally you'd pass, but since you're eager to have that type of client in your portfolio, you pursue it. Or perhaps you're experiencing a slow freelancing season and are eager for work, so you decide to move forward and develop a proposal.

Is the client ready to undertake the project?

Design is ultimately a collaboration. If you feel as though the client is unable to give the time, money, or attention to the project, no matter how good you are at your job, the project will not succeed without their effort too.

A few years ago, some of my family members purchased a campground resort that they wanted to rebrand. They were eager to refresh the look of the business the first summer they owned it. While I understood their desire to get right to work, I knew the design solution might not be effective if we did; they needed to become more familiar with the business—the clientele, the day-to-day challenges, and long-term goals—to gather more data to make the rebrand worth their investment. While it was hard to push them off, I knew it would yield better results later. After their first year owning the business, when we finally kicked off the project, they had more insights to share and use to make informed decisions. I'm confident waiting was the right decision for everyone involved.

Is there anything about the potential client that gives me pause?

If you feel a sense of hesitation, question why. Perhaps the thing that's giving you pause is not a reason to turn the potential project down, but instead indicates how you need to propose working with them. For example, the potential client during the "first date" phase has seemed very needy with lots of emails and questions at all times of day. While this might seem annoying, it's workable—you'll need to either set very clear boundaries around communication and/or charge this client more for the additional energy they will require. However, my best advice is to listen to your gut. If after the "first date" phase you strongly feel this is not a good fit, it probably isn't.

If the project is a good fit, you'll move to Chapter 3, "If you want to pursue the project."

If the project isn't right for you, you'll move to the next section in this chapter: "If you do not want to pursue the project."

If you do not want to pursue the project

It might feel like you're letting someone down by saying no. However, by turning down projects that are not a good fit, you're making space for projects that are. Trust yourself and do not be afraid to pass on an opportunity.

Let them know as soon as possible

If you know that this project is not right for you, let the potential client know straight away. That way, they have as much time as possible to find a better fit to meet their needs and their deadline.

Give them a recommendation

Here's the opportunity to pay it forward to another designer. This is another reason why having a network of trusted designers is useful.

Use ready-made replies that keep the door open for future collaborations

Even if the potential client is someone you think you'll never ever want to work for ever, ever, ever ... be nice about exiting the opportunity. Do not burn bridges—you never know where the potential client might pop up again. Your rejection email should demonstrate that you're not taking on the project because it's best *for them*. Below, I include a sample with some "excuses" to insert:

Name,

Thank you so much for thinking of me for your design project! After careful consideration, I unfortunately will not be able to take it on.

- *I'm currently at capacity for projects, and I could not give yours the time and attention it deserves.*
- *After reviewing your project needs, I do not think my design expertise is the best fit to meet your goals.*
- *I want to respect the budget you outlined, and my project minimum for (insert service / deliverable) is (insert number).*

A few other designers I recommend reaching out to are (insert information). Good luck on your project – looking forward to seeing how it comes together in the future!

Best,
Meaghan

If you've turned down a project, return to Chapter 1, "If you need to find a freelance project," to help you land other freelancing opportunities.

Interview

Arroz Con Pollo

Nabil Nadifi is the founder of Arroz Con Pollo, a creative studio based in Marrakesh, Morocco, Africa that specializes in strategy, branding, creative production, and education. While his client list ranges from local to global brands, a theme has emerged in his portfolio: showcasing his fellow Moroccans. For example, Nabil has collaborated with Marrakesh-based High Atlas Harvest Festival that promotes food sovereignty and the Foundation for the Safeguarding of Rabat's Cultural Heritage to celebrate the tenth anniversary of the Moroccan city's UNESCO World Heritage Designation.

Through *Arroz Con Pollo*, Nabil advocates for his community one project at a time. "Morocco is a country filled with creativity, but there's also a want and a need for Moroccan creatives to uplift each other," Nabil says. A country subjected to colonialism, Morocco's history continues to impact its present: "There are remnants of our colonial past, like coded beliefs that a designer who has studied in Europe is better than one who graduated from a Moroccan university. Creatives from here are still struggling. They have the same talent as French and UK designers, but are

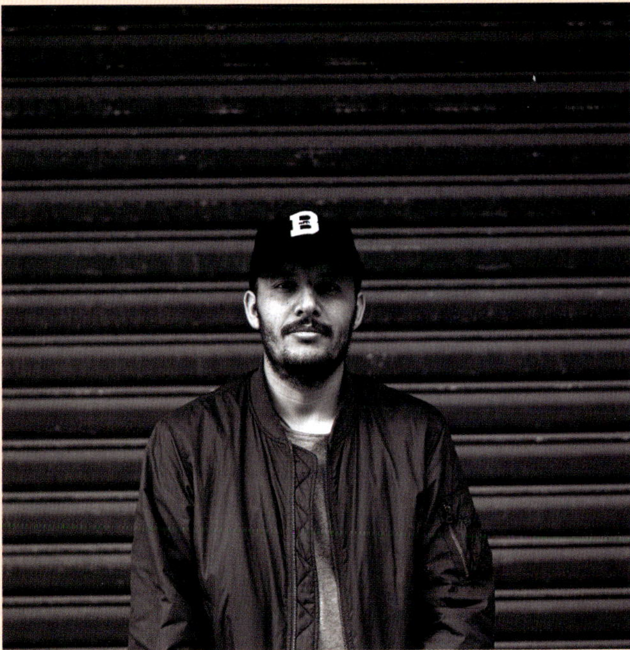

Figure 2.8 Nabil Nadifi of Arroz Con Pollo. Image courtesy of Nabil Nadifi.

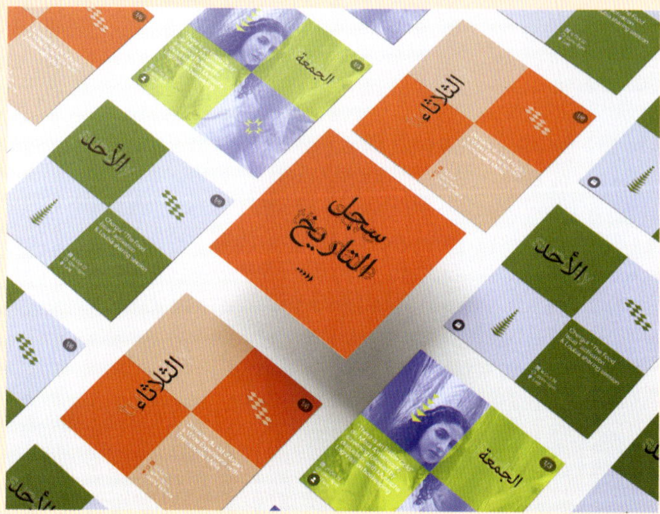

Figure 2.9 Arroz Con Pollo produced visual assets for Harvest Marrakech, including the fall edition's poster and program, social media content, and other print collateral. Image courtesy of Nabil Nadifi.

overlooked for opportunities." As a visual storyteller and a business owner, Nabil uses his expertise to shift these harmful perceptions: "I try to show that we have excellent Moroccan photographers, designers, and women creatives. As a Creative Director of my own studio, I hire local people to help me produce projects to prove that. These types of barriers maybe have broken down elsewhere, but in Morocco, we're still playing catch up."

Nabil serves as an example that your work, even seemingly small projects, can have positive social and cultural impacts. While it might feel overwhelming to tackle deeply embedded issues related to race, class, gender, and more while simultaneously meeting a client's deadline, let him inspire you to try. In Nabil's words, "No dream is too big."

Be a dreamer

Like many Moroccans, Nabil felt he had to study abroad to have a successful design career: he moved to Paris, France to receive his degree in advertising with a specialization in copywriting. After graduation, he worked full-time at various agencies throughout Europe. At his mid-year and annual reviews in his last corporate position, Nabil felt like he was never good enough: "It was like five minutes of praise, and then fifty-five minutes of how they expected me to do a lot more or else they'd give my job to someone else."

Once in a team-building exercise, Nabil and his colleagues were asked to fill out a questionnaire. Based on their answers, they were assigned a "corporate personality type" that was publicly shared with the group. "My persona was 'Dreamer.' All the others, like 'Workaholic' or 'Team Player,' made 'Dreamer' seem like the worst one. 'Dreamers' were depicted as unfocused and always late on assignments. I took it really personally being perceived that way in a room full of colleagues. It felt intrusive and embarrassing." After the event, he brought up the negative connotations of the word "dreaming" with his manager, and they brushed him off. "In that meeting, I actually said, 'I feel like it's accurate. Maybe that is me. I don't like the depiction of it in that little exercise, but perhaps a dreamer like me should not stay in a corporate environment.'" Nabil handed in his official resignation a few weeks later.

After quitting, he began freelancing for clients in Europe and the United States he acquired through his network, but eventually Nabil returned to Morocco to build Arroz Con Pollo. By going solo, he realized he did possess the professional skills he was told he lacked. "In my corporate job, I felt clumsy. They made me feel disorganized, unprofessional, and out of place." Nabil describes how he felt set up to fail in those roles, where he was overburdened with tasks and too many emails. Now, he has more freedom to implement his big ideas and manage his day to day in a way that works for him. "Running my own studio, I'm serious with my clients. I'm organized. I get to my emails on time because I'm not getting hundreds of useless ones a day. I'm proud of myself for realizing I just didn't fit into that specific corporate environment."

Nabil says being a "dreamer" has been an asset at Arroz Con Pollo: "Whoever's reading this, dreaming is not a bad word. Dreaming is a beautiful world." For instance, by volunteering to "dream up" a creative strategy for a local friend, he later landed a big international client, Audi:

> **I am friends with the editor of *Diptyk* magazine, the foremost printed publication about contemporary art in North Africa. She often complained how it was hard to balance running both the creative side of the magazine, as well as the business side where she was chasing clients and ad space. I took it upon myself to develop a branding or revenue stream strategy for her in hopes of alleviating her stress.**

In his pitch for her, he benchmarked cool, profitable magazines and suggested a rebrand for *Diptyk*. He also suggested using other mediums to output more content, like video production, newsletters, and a podcast. His editor friend agreed with his proposed plan, and they hired the editor's cousin, a graphic designer in Morocco, to refresh the visual look of the magazine.

At the same time, *Diptyk* was planning to cover an upcoming contemporary art fair in Marrakech called *1-54*. Nabil suggested approaching one of their existing clients who bought ad space in the magazine to ask them to sponsor a video about the

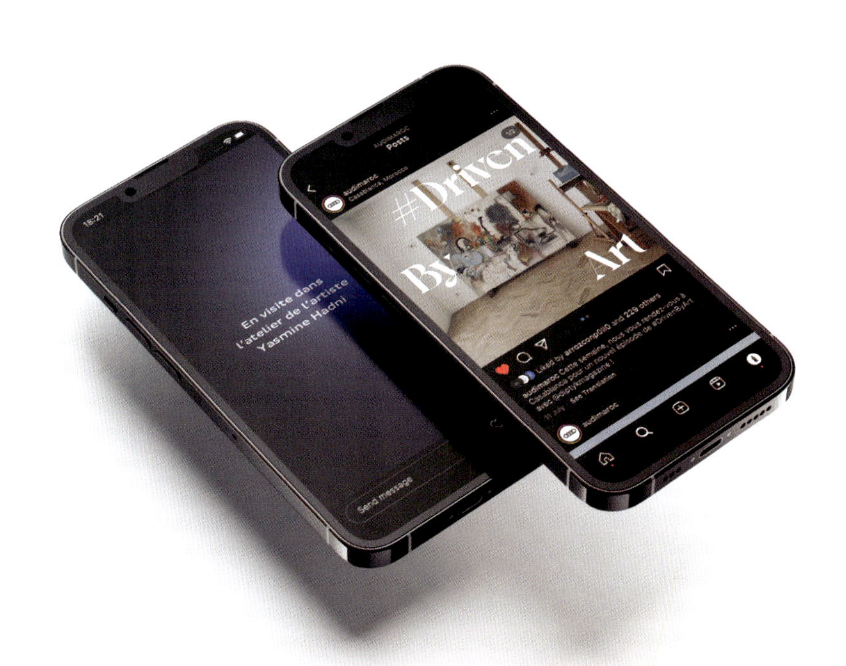

Figure 2.10 Each episode of *Driven By Art* is accompanied by a set of social media assets to complete the experience with exclusive photographs, quotes from guests, and outtakes. Image courtesy of Nabil Nadifi.

event. They inquired with Audi, and they agreed. Nabil reworked the initial concept of the video to include Audi cars, rather than a simple reporting of the art event. When Audi saw positive results from the three-part mini documentary produced by Arroz Con Pollo, they wanted to do more. For the latest project, they have Moroccan creatives and artists hopping into the luxury car and driving to locations throughout the North African country.

By genuinely investing in the success of *Diptyk*, a smaller local client and friend, Nabil was introduced to a larger, global client. He dreamed up alternative paths for the magazine that became successful realities for everyone involved. "It was not my strategy to land a new big account when I pitched those initial ideas to my editor friend, but that's how it happened."

Start a passion project

Nabil was comfortable freelancing because he started managing independent projects as a university student. After his father gifted him a camera for school, he started an online photo journal, which at the time was new for the internet. Nabil was an early online influencer; he would take photographs of exhibitions and events he'd go to on the weekends, which inspired others to do the same: "Classmates would tell me they'd checked out something because they saw about it on my blog."

After consistently posting his photography online, he began to get noticed by different brands, such as Nike, who'd invite him to parties in Paris. At those events, he was able to make connections with people in the creative industry. His passion project had grown into a professional opportunity.

As an offshoot of his blog, Nabil also became an early adopter of Facebook to post original content. "I didn't learn any of the social media aspects of my career in school. I learned as I was doing it." At his first full-time agency job, he'd initially been hired as a copywriter, but when they noticed he had a successful blog, they offered him a higher paying role to manage their social media.

Self-driven projects such as these have consistently created opportunities for Nabil throughout his career. Most recently, Nabil used his casual basketball league with "friends who've aged out of playing at a high frequency and intensity" to connect his passions with his work. When the group entered a tournament to play for fun, they had to come up with a team name to register. Nabil decided to use this as an exercise in branding and a break from his client work. He thought, "Let me do a logo for it. Next time we play, we'll have our own jerseys, T-shirts, an Instagram, and stuff like that." He built out the visual identity and products for La Ferraille Basketball Community.

The project has created meaningful connections for Nabil, including internationally, because his designs gave credibility and legitimacy to the group.

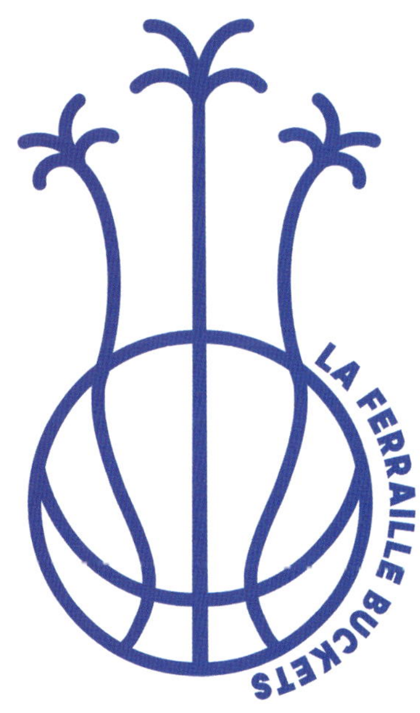

Figure 2.11 Logo designed by Nabil Nadifi for Morocco-based basketball community La Ferraille whose tagline is "Let the children hoop." Image courtesy of Nabil Nadifi.

I met people in Kuwait and in Canada who are doing similar stuff. We've exchanged clothing and basketballs we've all designed. I've gotten to play with people in London I was introduced to through La Ferraille's community. That group was great because they have sessions where everyone is welcome to play, no matter who you identify as. And even though our Instagram only has 300 or so followers, one is a former NBA [National Basketball Association in North America] player.

The project that started as a side hobby for fun is growing: "I can't say much now, but it's getting turned into an actual business."

These passion projects are iterations of Nabil's dreaming come to fruition. He says, "Dreaming doesn't have to be this gigantic unattainable thing. I love design and photography, and I also love basketball. La Ferraille is a mix of those passions, which feels obvious. Sometimes your dream doesn't have to be complicated."

Take on less work to do better work

For new freelancers, Nabil advises to be mindful of your time. "I realized that my commodity, the product I'm selling, is as much my expertise as my time. If you don't realize you're also selling time, you'll overwork yourself and eventually burn out." Nabil described a scenario where undervaluing your time can snowball into larger issues:

Your instinct might be to underprice yourself in order to land a project, but then you have to take on more jobs in order to pay your bills. Then you're so overbooked with low-paying jobs, which means you're rushing and likely not delivering an excellent product. That leads to unhappy clients, which means less return business from them and missing out on recommendations to their networks. Sometimes things that we think are helping us in the moment, are actually hurting us long term.

He suggests pricing your work by considering how much a half day or a full day of your work costs, and to be very honest about how much work goes into each project. He says to remember, "As you grow, so will your project budgets. If you add illustrators, video editors, or other creatives to accomplish the project, you will have to charge more." While designers cannot always control what project opportunities come their way, Nabil acknowledges setting boundaries in any scenario is important.

At first, it can be hard to know what you'll do for free or low-pay, what you'll be flexible on, and what you'll be strict on. For instance, all my clients, even my friends, have to pay us a deposit in advance. Then they pay us again upon delivery of the work. I say this as though making and following a rule like this is simple, but it's fifteen years in the making.

Nabil says copyright is also something to consider: "How long does a client have the right to own your work? Just because you're making something for someone does not mean they get to use it forever."

Get out of your algorithm bubble
The biggest piece of advice Nabil has for emerging designers is to increase your visual literacy by expanding your sources of inspiration.

If you're interested in graphic design, don't only look at graphic design books and Instagram accounts. You'll get more stimulation from watching a movie, reading a book, visiting an architectural site, listening to a podcast, rather than consuming only the same online design experts. Internet algorithms create sameness and loops that are intended to keep you logged on to an app, not to challenge you.

Nabil says in his own practice he's been returning to his childhood joys, such as reading manga, to push out of creative blocks.

One way many designers reinvigorate their creativity is through traveling. For those wanting to go to Morocco, Nabil says, "You are most welcome. The more the merrier. The more diverse voices we can have, that's great. However, if you're creative and want to come to Morocco to work, don't be a taker. Don't be a savior. Come here with that in mind."

To learn more about Nabil and Arroz Con Pollo:

Arrozconpollo.studio
@arrozconpOllO

3

If you want to pursue the project

Developing a proposal

You've gone on your "first date" (or maybe a few) with a potential client, and you're ready to make it official. The next step is to make your proposal. While you might not get down on one knee and present the potential client with an engagement ring, it is like you're asking for their hand in business. Your proposal outlines how you envision your future working together on the design project. It also functions like a prenuptial agreement, so in case you move forward together, but later decide to break up, there are pre-established rules in place to protect both of your interests.

What is a proposal?

A proposal is a multipage document that outlines the project scope (deliverables, timeline, pricing, etc.) and presents your vision for how you and the potential client will collaborate together to get the job done. It pitches your services to the client and is your competitive bid to convince the client to select you for the opportunity over other designers. However, it is much more than that.

It is a tool to protect both you and the client

Sometimes, proposals can make folks nervous; multiple pages with legal language would make me jumpy too. This is why it's important to emphasize to your potential client that a proposal is intended to protect both of you. If accepted, it holds the designer *and* the client accountable for their responsibilities throughout the project. If one does not meet the duties set out in the document, the other can use the agreement to hold them responsible. However, if you do not have the expectations for the project in writing, it will be challenging to come to a resolution.

It is negotiable

When you send off the proposal, think of it as your first offer. Be ready for the potential client to counter. They might want to negotiate the price, the timeline, or a detail in the terms and conditions.

It is a sales tool

A proposal can help you land more projects and justify a higher rate for your services if it presents a value-add to the client. For instance, a potential client who is new to the design process might select the proposal that was most organized, easy-to-understand, and welcoming. Another potential client might select the proposal that highlights the designer is bilingual, while a different client might select the proposal that is the most aesthetically pleasing. You need to use the information you gather in the "first date" phase to determine how to best pitch your services and yourself to that particular client in the proposal. Remember, value and price are not the same; being the cheapest designer does not mean you are offering the most value to the client. Consider how your proposal's content and design will promote your professionalism, customer service skills, and unique offerings to help sell your services.

It follows a formula

While proposals vary because every project is a little different, they follow the same basic setup (outlined in "Key elements of a proposal," later in this chapter). Writing these documents can be very labor-intensive, so I highly recommend developing a template. The proposal template does not need to be over-designed, but it should look like it came from a designer. As a potential client, if the proposal looks like a mess, I'm not sure I would trust that designer to create something for me. Instead, the template's design should emphasize the reader's needs, such as employing visual hierarchy and legible typefaces that make content easy to navigate and comprehend. The template should also be quick for you to update, so you do not have to think about the design each time you write a proposal. Instead, you can focus on accurately defining and communicating the project scope, and getting it sent off to the client.

I keep a folder on my laptop that includes every proposal I've written—every single one. Even if I do not get the project, I keep the proposal on file. This way, if a new project opportunity comes along that is similar, I can reference and/or borrow language from a previous proposal to save time. Anything you can do to make developing proposals more efficient without losing quality, do so; remember, proposals are an uncompensated form of labor.

If agreed to by both parties, a proposal will become a guide and a legal agreement for the duration of the project

Once you've both signed and dated the proposal, your business relationship is official. The proposal will be your guidebook throughout the project. Use the timeline.

Follow the payment schedule. Meet the project goals. The proposal is a useless document unless you implement it throughout the duration of the project.

You can edit the proposal details once the project kicks off, if agreed to by both parties. At some point throughout the design process, things will come up that deviate from what you initially agreed to in the proposal. If this happens, you can create an *addendum—an add-on to an agreement that outlines updates and changes.* You can capture the changes in a formal document that everyone signs, dates, and gets tacked on to the original proposal. Minor changes, such as a size change for a deliverable or a deadline extension, that are easily agreeable can be documented in email. Ensure the email captures the proposed update(s) and both parties' approval, making it easy to reference later if necessary.

See Figures 3.1–3.9 for a sample proposal using examples featured in the following sections.

Key elements of a proposal

- Cover letter
- Project goals
- Project deliverables
- Project timeline
- Pricing
- Payment schedule
- Portfolio link or samples
- Terms and conditions
- Signature(s)

How to gather information for a proposal

You should have done this work when you completed the "first date" phase in Chapter 2, "If someone is interested in working with you." *If you didn't do this yet, return there.* The information you gathered on that "first date" with the potential client matters now. You're going to use that information to develop your proposal.

Cover letter writing for freelancing

When applying for jobs, a cover letter's purpose is to convince an employer to interview you. However, as a freelancer, you're usually writing a design proposal after a potential client has already "interviewed" you in the "first date" phase. If you've had a personal touchpoint with the potential client already—emails, calls, or meetings—a cover letter becomes less critical because you've already been able to introduce and pitch yourself. In this scenario, the email you send with your proposal will serve as a condensed cover letter. An example of what my email to the potential client might be is:

"Name",

It was so great to learn more about your coffee shop last week – our neighborhood is lucky to have you! As discussed, I've included a proposal below that outlines how I can help you meet your goals by redesigning your current website. Do not hesitate to reach out with questions or concerns. Thanks again for the consideration, and looking forward to continuing the conversation.

Best,
Meaghan

I recommend writing a formal cover letter if:

- ***You are applying for an RFP*** (see "Local community," in Chapter 2). In most RFP processes, you have no interaction with the potential client. This cover letter gives you an opportunity to "speak" to them and convince them why they should select you for the next phase of their RFP process.
- ***You want to further pitch yourself to the potential client.*** Sometimes in the "first date" interactions, there is a limited amount of time to sell yourself. If there are additional things you feel like the potential client must know that you did not mention or want to emphasize, a cover letter is a great place to include this information.
- ***Your proposal will go to a team of people.*** If you are proposing a project to more than one person, including a cover letter ensures everyone "hears" the same pitch from you. Your "voice" travels with the cover letter if it is embedded within the proposal. For example, imagine you email the proposal to your initial project contact, Fernando, who you gathered information from in the "first date." Then Fernando sends your proposal to his colleagues Shelby, Mark, and Reed, who you have not met yet, but they are decision-makers on the project. Luckily, you included a cover letter, so even though those three folks haven't had a personal interaction with you, they get an idea of who you are and what you're offering them. This way, you do not have to rely on Fernando to solely advocate for you.

For formal cover letters, keep it short—no longer than one page should be needed. You can use a template to make the process more efficient. A basic formula of core elements to include are:

1. An introduction that grabs the reader's attention.
2. An overview of the problem the potential client is looking to solve.
3. A pitch for why you're a great selection for their design challenge.
4. An action-oriented wrap-up.

Keep the focus on the potential client and their needs through the letter—make them the "hero" of the story. One way to do this is by repeating words and phrases the potential client used in your "first date" interactions or in their RFP—this demonstrates you were listening to them (and will make your writing easier). I recommend mirroring the formality of the potential client in your writing style; if they seem very serious, use more proper language, while if they appear more laid-back, use more casual language.

Set objective goals

Project goals should not feel like a repeat of the project deliverables with the words "design a ... " in front of it. For instance, "design a new website" is *not* a good project goal. A better project goal will establish criteria for whether your new website design is successful or not. Of course, at the end of the project, we want our clients to be happy with our work. However, "making the client happy" is also *not* a good project goal because it is too subjective. There is no way to measure if your client is "happy enough" with your work. This is why the best project goals are objective.

Let's see why in an example:

> During the "first date" phase, the potential client expressed that their current website frustrates them. They feel like it is "hard to navigate, too cluttered, and outdated" and "want it to be more modern." Their coffee shop regularly hosts events in the evenings and the potential client "cannot easily update the website to promote these to their customers." The majority of their customers are "students who attend the university in town." The potential client gave you a lot of excellent and juicy information to work with there. Imagine for your project goal you write:
>
> - Design a modern website that is easy to update for the business owner.

Sounds okay based on your initial conversation, right? Let's fast forward to when you've been working on the project. You've sent the client the final invoice for the website design. Even though you felt like the process went well, the client surprises you by refusing to pay. Their reason is because they "Don't like how the site looks. It's not modern at all!" But what does "modern" actually mean? As a subjective term, the client and you could have very different visions for what a "modern" website is. The two of you could argue over the meaning ad nauseum and never come to a resolution. *(Side note: if a client does use subjective terms such as "modern," ask them follow-up questions. For instance, "Can you show me some businesses that feel modern to you and tell me why?" By having them provide a visual example that you can look at together, it will help you understand what they mean.)*

Let's go back in time and rewrite the project goals to be more objective. The project goals you propose now are:

- Optimize the online customer experience through simplifying the site's navigation and reducing redundant information.
- Improve the website's responsiveness, as the target audience of university students primarily access the site on their mobile devices.
- Raise awareness about the store's events to increase attendance.
- Reduce the time for the business owner to update frequently changing website content such as seasonal menus and upcoming events.

Suddenly, the client's pushback about the site not looking "modern" falls apart because the project goals are less subjective. With these goals in place, you could reply to the client:

> *I'm sorry to hear that you're disappointed with how the website looks. However, based on the proposal, I've fulfilled my responsibilities we agreed to as outlined in the project goals. For example, the website is now fully responsive, and your events are now featured at the top of the homepage. If you'd like me to explain how else I met my project obligations, I'm happy to continue the conversation. Otherwise, I'll expect payment by the end of the month as agreed to.*

By setting objective goals in the proposal before the project begins, it:

- ***Gives you the opportunity to revise the project goals before agreeing to work together.*** If you and the client are not on the same page, revisit your "first date" phase conversations, realign your expectations with one another, and update the proposal. And if you cannot agree, everyone can go their separate ways before the project has even started.
- ***Reduces personal opinions from decision-making, which can often derail design projects from meeting their goals.*** Clients *and designers* often forget that their personal taste—subjective data—is not the sole focus when making design choices. Creating pleasing aesthetics is crucial, but solving the project's challenges is essential. Throughout the design process, you and your client can return to the objective goals to keep you on task. For instance, imagine your client is a forty-something-year-old coffee shop owner whose primary clientele is twenty-something students in a college town. If the owner begins to provide feedback such as, "I don't like it," you can dig in deeper and ask them why. If they respond that it's based on their personal taste, you can kindly acknowledge their viewpoint, but bring the conversation back to the fundamental goal: *Will their twenty-something coffee shop customers like it based on your research?* The client's opinion absolutely matters, but it's critical to the project's success that the design caters to their target audience.
- ***Provides measurable ways to determine success.*** If a scenario does arise where a client feels like you did not meet your end of the bargain, you will be able to provide factual and evidence-based reasons to defend your position, which will be harder to argue with.

Why deliverable specificity matters

A client comes to you and says, "I want a website design." Great! Imagine in your proposal you list:

Project deliverables:

- Website Design, $1,000

In your mind, $1,000 is a fair price (*more about pricing soon in "How to price your work," in this chapter—go with me here for now*) because a website design will be simple. The client agrees to the proposal, and you begin the project. However, as it goes on, you realize that the client's expectations for a website design are much different from what you anticipated: they actually want a website design with e-commerce. The client is eager to increase their business revenue through internet sales, but you did not account for including an online shop in your proposal. You know this is much more work than what you initially thought would be a few static website pages.

The problem is that you've left yourself too much gray area in the language of your proposal. If you approach the client now for more money to complete the e-commerce portion of website, your argument will be harder to make. The client could say, "You agreed to a 'website design.' This is a website design." Of course, you can explain the additional work to the client, but there is a lot of potential for that conversation to get messy.

Alright, so perhaps instead you should have written in your proposal:

Project deliverables:

- Website Design with E-Commerce, $5,000

While that might seem better, there's still an issue. Any guesses?

Here's the answer: Setting up an e-commerce site for ten products is very different than setting up an e-commerce site that offers 1,000 products. To do the math very simply:

- $5,000 total project price / 10 e-commerce products = $500 per product to setup on the site
  vs
- $5,000 total project price / 1,000 e-commerce products = $5.00 per product to setup on the site

Without outlining how many products are included, you again set yourself up for an awkward conversation with your client and the potential to lose a lot of money. The more labor intensive the project, the more you should be charging.

In your proposal, you want to be as specific about the deliverables as possible. Here's a better example of how you could outline the website design project in your proposal.

Project deliverables:

- Website Design, $5,000
- The website will be built using the Squarespace platform. The designer will use Squarespace's built-in website builder tools. This estimate does not include custom coding or development.
- The website design will include an e-commerce shop. The designer will build the shop to include forty (40) product SKUs.
    - *The reason I am now using the term "SKU" which stands for "Stock Keeping Unit" is that it indicates an individual specific product. No two products can have the same SKU number. The word "product" alone indicates something general such as a "shirt," which again, creates a lot of gray area in language, whereas a "product SKU" indicates a child's T-shirt that is a size small and the color blue.*

See how much more specific I'm being? This way, if the client begins to *scope creep, which is when the project requirements increase or change beyond what you initially agreed to*, it will be easier to advocate for yourself. Imagine now if the client says, "I need to add an additional ten product SKUs to the site," you will be able to say, "I'd love to help you with that. Since our initial proposal only quoted for forty, the additional ten will cost another $1,250 and it will add a week to the timeline. If this works for you, I will add an addendum to our proposal and will send you an invoice for the additional work." Perhaps the client wants a special feature that is not included as a standard offering in the Squarespace platform. You could say, "That's a great idea to include that feature on the site! Unfortunately, Squarespace does not offer that without custom coding and that's not my area of expertise. However, I'd be happy to put you in touch with a developer who could help make that happen for you."

These conversations suddenly become *much* easier to have with a client because what you initially agreed to design was clear and detailed in the proposal. In reality, most projects are going to shift a little along the way—it is not the client being outwardly greedy or malicious. This is why when you outline the project deliverables, include every possible detail you can—the size of print pieces, the length of a video, the number of pages of a book—because this will allow you to use your proposal as a negotiation tool as changes emerge.

Creating a realistic timeline

An effective timeline is more than a list of dates and deadlines; it functions as an organized to-do list, broken up into phases throughout a project. It keeps both the designer and the client responsible for a successful outcome. When developing your timeline, it is important to:

- ***Always start with a project kick-off meeting.*** This step is important because sometimes you sign off on the proposal in January, but you do not start the project until April. In those months, some things might have shifted in the client's project. By having the kick-off meeting right at the beginning, it gives you a chance to renegotiate or edit the proposal if any big changes have occurred in that period. I'll discuss the kick-off meeting more in Chapter 4, "Working together."

- ***Account for more than just design time.*** As a freelancer, there is more to do than sit at your computer and design. Your timeline should account for all the time—thinking time, emailing time, meeting time, editing time, client feedback time—that goes into the project. With some of these tasks being harder to estimate, especially when you're new, always build in extra time. It is better to be early or on-time for a deadline, than late. One way to become better at estimating your time is to begin tracking it while you work. Use a time tracker (there are many free online versions) and log all your time in categories—and be honest. Sometimes I feel like I've been working all afternoon, when in reality, a good chunk of time I was actually scrolling on social media. Through this exercise, you quickly learn where you spend your time—and if that might need to change.
- ***Outline both the designer's and the client's responsibilities.*** A common mistake emerging designers make when developing their timeline is they only include what they are responsible for. However, the design process is collaborative, and the designer is not the only person with tasks to accomplish to make sure it goes smoothly. Remember, many of your clients will be beginners to the design process and unsure of their role. By including the client's responsibilities, the timeline becomes an educational tool for them about how they impact deadlines.

  A designer's responsibilities in a timeline may include, but are not limited to:
  - Design-related tasks such as developing initial ideas, implementing edits, and finalizing files for production
  - Project management tasks such as scheduling meetings and sending invoices
  - Collaborating with other design teams and project vendors.

  A client's responsibilities in a timeline may include, but are not limited to:
  - Providing the designer with information and content
  - Offering the designer feedback
  - Making a scheduled payment.

For example, before you can begin designing, there are often key pieces of information you need from your client to get started. An early phase of the project might look something like this:

PHASE 1B—STRATEGY & CONTENT ACQUISITION

The Designer will conduct research about current industry website trends and review competitor sites. The Designer will prepare a presentation to share their findings and recommendations.

The Client must provide the items listed below to the Designer before the project can move to Phase 2:

- o Website login information
- o New website content (proofed text and images)
- o Brand identity files (logo files, color and font information, etc.)

The Client can share these with the Designer via email, Google Drive, Dropbox, or another file transfer site.

- ***Break it into phases that align with actions.*** By creating phases tied to actions, ones that build over time to fulfill the project goals, the timeline functions like a to-do list. At every point in the design process, you and the client will know what needs to happen and when. It also helps that if an action does not happen, it provides a "stop gap" to pause the project until everyone has completed their checklist. Check Figure 2.1, "Timeline of a project" (page 43), to see how this works in context of the larger project. This is especially important for you in the event a client "ghosts" you throughout the project, which unfortunately happens. For instance:
  - o If a client does not provide the information you need to do your job, you do not continue to the next phase until they do.
  - o If a client does not provide feedback in the scheduled time frame, you do not continue to the next phase until they do.
  - o If a client does not pay the next scheduled payment installment, you do not continue to the next phase until they do.

In your timeline, it is important that the client has a certain amount of time assigned to their tasks too. Imagine that a client disappears for weeks, but then comes back suddenly three days before the initially proposed project deadline and is still expecting you to meet it. Luckily, you wrote your timeline like this:

PHASE 2C—DESIGN EDIT TWO

The Designer will provide the Client with an updated design to review via email based on Phase 2B feedback. Once received, the Client must provide feedback within one week of receiving the design file. The project will not move to Phase Three until feedback has been received. If feedback is received after the deadline, the proposed timeline is subject to change, or a rush fee may be instituted.

For an example of a full project timeline, see the proposal sample on pgs 84–92 (Figures 3.1 through 3.9).

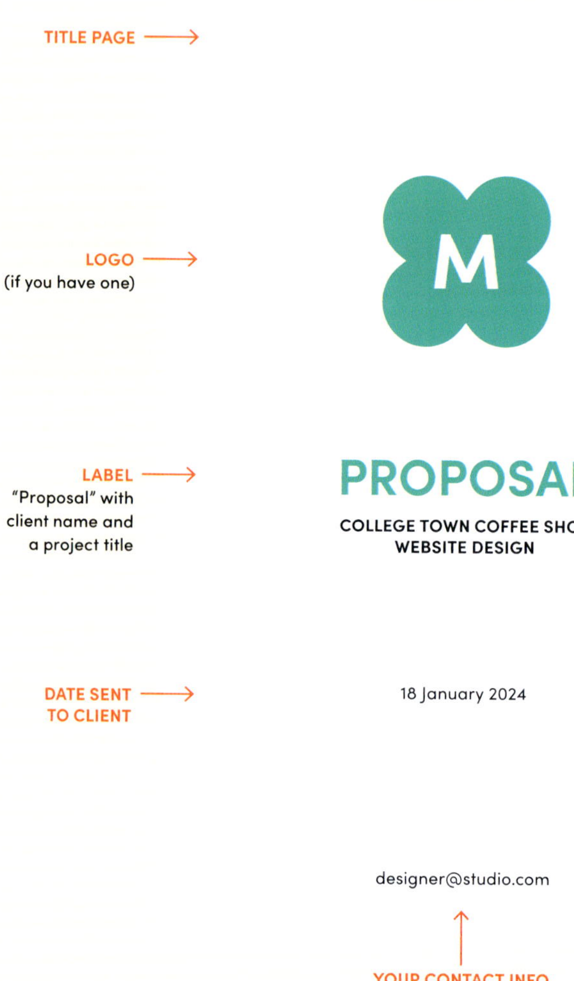

Figure 3.1 Sample proposal, page 1.

PROPOSAL EXAMPLE

PAGE TWO

COVER LETTER →

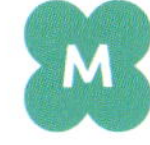

Hello Kimmie,

INTRODUCTION → It was great to chat with you and learn more about your website needs at College Town Coffee Shop last week. I'm still thinking about the homemade scones you shared with me that day – so delicious! Thank you again for hosting me.

CLIENT NEEDS → I understand your frustrations with your current website; it does not accurately reflect the high-quality service and charm of your business. Through a new website design, we will modernize your online customer experience and better engage with your primary audience: local university students. We will focus on making the new site user-friendly, reducing clutter, and highlighting your products through an e-commerce shop.

YOUR PITCH → I spent many late nights at College Town Cofee Shop while studying for my degree in graphic design, sipping on maple lattes and listening to talented musicians from our community at your events. Now, I want to use my expertise to ensure folks continue to benefit from your business. As a recent alumni from the local university, I'm in tune with the wants and needs of your target audience. Combined with my experience as a customer, I'm confident I can deliver a great website design that meets your goals.

WRAP-UP → Looking forward to continuing the conversation with you! I'll follow up in the next couple of weeks, but if you have any questions or concerns in the meantime, please reach out.

Cheers!

Meaghan

designer@studio.com

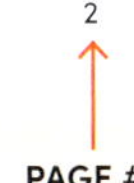

PAGE #

Figure 3.2 Sample proposal, page 2.

PROPOSAL EXAMPLE

PAGE THREE

SECTION HEADERS Keep this document organized and easy for the reader to find information.

PROJECT GOALS

STRATEGY & DESIGN

- Optimize the online customer experience through simplifying the site's navigation and reducing redundant information.
- Improve the website's responsiveness, as the target audience of university students primarily access the site on their mobile devices.
- Raise awareness about the store's events to increase attendance.
- Create an online shop to sell branded products to customers.
- Reduce the time for the business owner to update frequently changing website content such as seasonal menus and events.

IMPLEMENTATION

- Launch the site to the public.
- Provide ongoing support once site is live.

PROJECT DELIVERABLES

WEBSITE DESIGN WITH E-COMMERCE

- The website will be built using the Squarespace platform. The Designer will use Squarespace's built-in website builder tools. This estimate does not include custom coding or development.

- The website design will include an e-commerce shop. The Designer will build the shop to include forty (40) product SKUs. The Client has identified products such as their roasted coffee beans, coffee tools, branded shop merchandise, and tickets to in-store events.

WEBSITE MAINTENANCE

- The Designer will perform ongoing website maintenance upon the Client's request. The Designer will perform updates that can be completed using Squarespace's built-in website builder tools. This estimate does not include requests that require custom coding or development.

3

Figure 3.3 Sample proposal, page 3.

PROPOSAL EXAMPLE

PAGE FOUR

PRO TIP Align project goals with the phases of the project timeline.

PRO TIP Write policies, like if deadlines are missed or how edits should be sent, as a "blanket" for the project so you do not have to repeat it over and over again in your project timeline.

PROJECT TIMELINE

PHASE 1: STRATEGY

Phase 1A: Kick-Off Meeting + Design Brief Creation
Schedule for week of 4 Feb 2024
One-hour meeting, plus two weeks for revisions

An in-person or online video chat project kick-off meeting will be scheduled. All Client decision-makers must be in attendance, or the meeting will be rescheduled. The Designer will send a questionnaire ahead of time that will guide the meeting conversation. After the meeting, the Designer will develop a Design Brief. The Client will have one week to review the document and provide feedback. If feedback is received after the deadline, the proposed timeline is subject to change, or a rush fee may be instituted. Throughout the project, the Client can send feedback and edits in writing in an email, or can schedule a phone or video call with the Designer to discuss. The Designer will implement feedback within one week and send to Client for approval. Once approved, the project will move to Phase 1B.

Phase 1B: Strategy & Content Acquisition
Two weeks

The Designer will conduct research about current industry website trends and review competitor sites. The Designer will prepare a presentation to share their findings and recommendations.

The Client must provide the items listed below to the Designer before the project can move to Phase 1C:

- website login information
- new website content (proofed text and images)
- brand identity files (logo files, color & font information, etc.)

The Client can share these with the Designer via email, Google Drive, Dropbox, or another file transfer site.

Phase 1C: Strategy Presentation
One-hour meeting, plus one week for feedback

An in-person or online video chat strategy presentation will be scheduled. All Client decision-makers must be in attendance. Designer will present findings from Phase 1B. Client must provide feedback within one week before moving to Phase 2.

4

Figure 3.4 Sample proposal, page 4.

PROPOSAL EXAMPLE

PAGE FIVE

PRO TIP → Avoid hard dates; if a Client (or you) get off the proposed schedule, it becomes more confusing. Instead, provide more general estimates for time required for that phase (hours, days, weeks, months).

PRO TIP → Be clear that the project will not move forward into the next phase unless an action has been completed.

PHASE 2: DESIGN

Phase 2A: Three Design Directions
Three weeks of design, one-hour meeting, plus one week for feedback

Designer will develop three different possible design solutions based on the strategy developed with Client in Phase 1. The Designer will present the varying directions to the Client in an in-person or online video chat. All Client decision-makers must be in attendance.

Immediately upon the meeting's conclusion, the Designer will provide the Client the presentation slides. Once received, the Client must provide feedback within one week of receiving the design file. The project will not move to Phase 2B until feedback has been received.

Phase 2B: Design Edit One
Two weeks of design, plus one week for feedback

The Designer will provide the Client with an up-to-date design to review via email based on Phase 2A feedback. Once received, the Client must provide feedback within one week of receiving the design file. The project will not move to Phase 2C until feedback has been received.

Phase 2C: Design Edit Two
Two weeks of design, plus one week for feedback

The Designer will provide the Client with an up-to-date design to review via email based on Phase 2B feedback. Once received, the Client must provide feedback within one week of receiving the design file. The project will not move to Phase 3 until feedback has been received.

PHASE 3: IMPLEMENTATION

Phase 3A: Final Design and Approval
One week of design, plus one week for approval

The Designer will implement final edits from Phase 2C and provide the Client with the final design. The Client has one week to approve the final design. If more requests are requested at this time, an hourly fee of $44/hour will be instituted. The project will not move to Phase 3B until final approval has been received via email.

5

Figure 3.5 Sample proposal, page 5.

PROPOSAL EXAMPLE

PAGE SIX

Phase 3B: Site Launch
One business day

Once final payment has been received (see Payment Schedule on page 6–7), the Designer will launch the site, making it accessible to the general public.

Phase 3C: Ongoing website maintenance
TBD

The Client must make requests ten (10) business days before the proposed deadline, otherwise the project may be subject to a "rush fee." The Designer will provide the Client a pricing estimate and project timeline based on the request.

Once approved by the Client, the Designer will begin implementing maintenance requests. The Designer will update the Client every five (5) hours of design work completed on these tasks.

PROJECT ESTIMATE

- WEBSITE DESIGN WITH E-COMMERCE, $5,000
- WEBSITE MAINTENANCE, $44/HOUR

PRO TIP →
Align your payment schedule with the phases of your project timeline.

PAYMENT SCHEDULE

PROJECT DEPOSIT, $2,500
Phase 1 will begin once 50% of total estimate for Website Design with E-Commerce has been received.

PAYMENT TWO, $1,500
Designer will invoice for payment upon completion of Phase 2B. Phase 2C will begin once payment has been paid in full.

FINAL PAYMENT, $1,000
Designer will invoice for payment upon completion of Phase 3A. Phase 3B will begin once payment has been paid in full

WEBSITE MAINTENANCE - TBD, HOURLY WORK
The Designer will invoice Client in five (5) hour increments, or upon completion and approval of maintenance requests – whichever occurs first.

6

Figure 3.6 Sample proposal, page 6.

PROPOSAL EXAMPLE

PAGE SEVEN

PRO TIP Make hyperlinks so the reader can click and go.

PORTFOLIO SAMPLE

GENERAL PORTFOLIO SITE

WEBSITE-SPECIFIC PROJECT SAMPLES
This link is password-protected. Password is: AuggieDoggy

PRO TIP Have one line at the beginning that identifies "Client" and "Designer" with the date. This way, you do not have to insert the client's name throughout the terms and conditions, which will save time.

TERMS AND CONDITIONS

This Agreement is effective as of **(18 January 2024)**, between **(College Town Coffee Shop)** ("Client") and **(M Designs)** ("Designer").

PROPOSAL
The terms of the Proposal is effective for thirty (30) days after presentation to Client. In the event this Agreement is not executed by Client within the time identified, the Proposal may be subject to change.

HOURS OF OPERATION
Monday through Friday, 9am–5pm Eastern Standard Time, unless otherwise communicated by the Designer in advance.

PROJECT EXPENSES
The Client shall pay the Designer's expenses incurred in connection with the project. The pricing estimate includes the Designer's fee only.
Any and all outside costs including, but not limited to: equipment rental, photography costs, developer's costs and fees, licenses (artwork, photography, fonts), production costs, and online hosting fees, will be billed to the Client in the final project payment.

PAYMENT TERMS
All invoices are due within thirty (30) days of receipt.

LATE FEES
A monthly service charge of 5 percent (5%) of the invoice is payable on all overdue balances. Designer reserves the right to withhold delivery and transfer of ownership of any current work if invoices are overdue or not paid in full.

7

Figure 3.7 Sample proposal, page 7.

PROPOSAL EXAMPLE

PAGE EIGHT

RUSH FEES
The Client must make project requests ten (10) business days before the proposed deadline, otherwise the project may be subject to a "rush fee," a 30% mark-up of non-rush project fees.

OWNERSHIP AND LICENSING
The Designer retains the right to reproduce, publish, and display the project deliverables in the Designer's portfolios and websites, and in other media or exhibits for the purpose of promotion and recognition.

License to use and/or transfer of ownership are on the condition of payment in full by the Client.

PROJECT CANCELLATION
This Agreement may be terminated at any time by either the Client or the Designer with seven (7) days notice to the other party. In the event of project cancellation, the Designer will be compensated for the services performed up until the date of cancellation, including expenses.

CATASTROPHIC EVENTS
Designer shall not be deemed in breach of this Agreement if the Designer is unable to complete the services or any portion by reason of a "Force Majeure Event." Upon occurrence of any Force Majeure Event, the Designer will give notice to the Client of its inability to perform or of delay in completing the services and will propose revisions to the schedule for completion of services.

DON'T FORGET TO SIGN & DATE
This is what makes this document legal!

PROPOSAL AND AGREEMENT ACCEPTED BY CLIENT

SIGNATURE:
PRINT NAME / TITLE:
DATE:

PROPOSAL AND AGREEMENT ACCEPTED BY DESIGNER

SIGNATURE:
PRINT NAME / TITLE:
DATE:

8

Figure 3.8 Sample proposal, page 8.

PROPOSAL ADDENDUM EXAMPLE

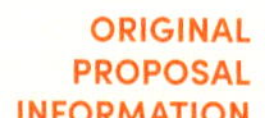

ORIGINAL PROPOSAL INFORMATION
Client name, project title, and proposal date

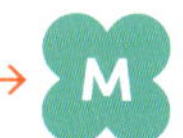

PROPOSAL ADDENDUM

COLLEGE TOWN COFFEE SHOP WEBSITE DESIGN
PROPOSAL DATED 18 JANUARY 2024

ADDITIONAL PROJECT DELIVERABLES

WEBSITE DESIGN
The Designer will build the shop to include twelve (12) additional product SKUs. The new total of SKUs is fifty-two (52).

EXTRA EDITS
The Client requested additional design edits after Phase 2C via email. The Designer will complete these requests at an hourly rate of $44/hour.

PROPOSED UPDATES
Think who, what, when, where, and why. If any of these changed, include it.

PROJECT TIMELINE CHANGES

EXTENSION OF PHASE 3A
An additional week will be added to Phase 3A for the Designer to add additional product SKUS to the site before moving to Phase 3B.

ADDITIONAL PROJECT COSTS

- TWELVE PRODUCT SKUS, $1,250
- EXTRA EDITS, Estimated 3 hours of design time, ~$132

The Designer will add these costs to the Final Payment invoice.

DON'T FORGET TO SIGN & DATE
This is what makes this document legal!

ADDENDUM ACCEPTED BY CLIENT

SIGNATURE:
PRINT NAME / TITLE:
DATE:

ADDENDUM ACCEPTED BY DESIGNER

SIGNATURE:
PRINT NAME / TITLE:
DATE:

A-1

PAGE #

Figure 3.9 Sample proposal, Addendum.

How to price your work

Ideally, the client has communicated a budget for you to create a pricing structure around. However, often they're looking to you to establish the project price.

I wish I could say pricing your work gets easier with time, but honestly, I still struggle with perfectly quoting for my design services. You quickly learn when you've underestimated or undervalued your work, and you'll remedy it the next time you propose a project. There are resources and books dedicated to pricing if you want to dig deeper into the subject—I'm a fan of *The Psychology of Graphic Design Pricing* by Michael Janda. Another resource is *The Graphics Artists Guild Handbook: Pricing & Ethical Guidelines* book that provides suggested price ranges for various design deliverables, with suggested market rates for your specific type of work and experience level. For now, I'm keeping it to the essentials to get you started on pricing your work.

Throughout this section, I feature sample rates in my examples. These are not recommendations for what you should charge for your work; instead, these figures were selected to keep the math fairly simple. There is no "one-size-fits-all" magic number to charge clients. You'll need to use the exercises to create price points that are personalized to you.

Different pricing models

Hourly rate

With this pricing model, you're paid a set amount for every hour you work. For example, if your hourly rate is $50/hour and you work ten hours, the project total is $500.

How to set an hourly rate: If you have no idea what your hourly rate should be, use the exercise below. There are other factors to consider, such as your personal and business expenses, however, if you're just starting out freelancing, this will provide you a baseline to start with.

1. Determine what the annual salary of a designer with your experience, in your location is. Perhaps based on your research, in a small city in the United States your market value is $75,000.
2. Take that annual salary and divide it by the total weeks in a year that you'd work at a full-time design job (let's say forty-nine, because you take three weeks of vacation):
   $75,000/49 = ~$1,530.61
3. Then, use that weekly rate and divide by the number of work hours in a week (let's say forty, a typical American workweek):
   ~$1,530.61/40 = $38/hour.
   This number is the minimum amount you should charge (in most cases) to ensure you're not losing money.

4. You'll want to include a profit margin (10–20 percent mark-up) on top of the minimum hourly rate. This will give you some wiggle room in negotiation with potential clients, as well as pad your savings account in case equipment breaks or other unexpected situations occur. In this scenario, let's say you want a 15 percent profit margin:
   $38 x 15% = $5.70, then $38 + $5.70 = $43.70/hour
5. Let's round up to a whole dollar amount:
   $44/hour will be a good baseline hourly rate.

Hourly rate advantages

- For the designer, this pricing model can feel less risky, especially if you have a demanding client or a project scope that is amorphous. If the client "scope creeps," for instance new deliverables are added, it does not matter because you are getting compensated for the amount of time you work.

Hourly rate challenges

- For the client, this pricing model can feel risky because it is harder for them to budget than a flat fee. They also need to trust the designer is being efficient during their working hours, and accurately reporting said hours. With these considerations, this pricing model can be a tougher sell to a potential client, especially one who is less familiar with the design process.
- This model caps your earning potential because it becomes tied to time; there are only so many working hours within a day. Let's say you want to work eight hours per day. If your hourly rate is $50/hour, this means your maximum earning potential is $400 per working day. However, imagine you take on a $400 flat fee project. You're a fast worker, and you complete the job within five hours. Suddenly, your hourly rate increases to $80/hour for that project, and three hours remain in your workday to do other tasks and earn more. Hourly models might be "safer," but it does not incentivize productivity, which can be a way to increase your revenue.
- Throughout the project, you have to be diligent about tracking your hours and writing a description of what you did within that time (i.e., meetings, designing, editing, emailing the client, etc.); everything that pertains to the client and the project must be tracked. I round up to the quarter of an hour, so if I had a meeting that lasted one hour and ten minutes, I round up to 1.25 hours, or if I designed for three hours and thirty-seven minutes, I round up to 3.75 hours for billing. The challenge is remembering to track; I have forgotten to turn on my timer, then lowball myself when I retroactively input the hours. I do this because I feel icky about the client potentially overpaying for my mistake.
- You need to regularly communicate with the client about your hours—just because they are paying you this way does not mean they have an endless supply of cash. Imagine you put twenty-five hours into a project, but never communicate with the client about that time. They might be in for a shock when you bill them for more than they anticipated, and conflict could emerge.

To avoid this, I recommend setting a standard "check-in" with the client, such as every five hours of work. You communicate that you've worked the agreed hours, then wait for their sign-off before continuing to the next increment. While this might slow the process down, at least this way, the client has the opportunity to say "This is getting too expensive for me. What are our options?" and you will not find yourself in a position where the client cannot afford to pay you at the end of the project.

Flat fee

With this pricing model, you're paid a specific sum for the total project, regardless of labor time. For example, if the project takes you two hours or ten hours to complete, the project total remains the same at $500.

How to determine a flat rate: *You must know your hourly rate before you can determine a flat rate. If you have not determined your hourly rate, go back and complete that step.*

1. Estimate the total number of hours you anticipate the project will take. This is not just your time sitting at your computer and designing; do not forget client contact time (phone calls, emails, meetings), research time, revision time, working with vendors such as printers, and so on. I encourage you to round up if you're unsure—you will likely take more time completing a task than you think. Let's say you've estimated designing a book cover will take twenty-four hours.
2. You will now multiply the estimated hours (24) by your hourly rate (let's use the $44/hour from the previous exercise):
   $44 x 24 = $1,056
3. Next, consider if there are any additional costs you anticipate associated with the project such as hiring help or renting equipment. As a new or part-time freelancer, you will often not have any additional costs. However, for the sake of the example, let's imagine you want to hire your illustrator friend to create hand-drawn text for the book cover. They plan to charge you $500 for their services. You need to add this extra cost:
   $1,056 + $500 = $1556

$1,556 represents your baseline flat fee. If you charge the client this amount and complete the work in the proposed twenty-four hours, you will be profitable. If you do the work faster (less than twenty-four hours) and/or charge more than the $1,556 at the outset, you increase your profitability. However, if you charge less than $1,556 and/or you work more than the proposed hours, you will be decreasing your profitability.

Flat fee advantages

- For the client, this pricing model is less risky because the total project price is determined at the beginning; they know exactly what they will receive from

you and for how much. This transparency alleviates stress, so a flat rate is likely an easier sell to the potential client.
- Productivity is incentivized, so if you work efficiently, your earning potential increases.

Flat fee challenges

- For the designer, this pricing model is riskier because you must accurately estimate your time to determine the flat rate and there is potential to under-price yourself. For many new freelancers, estimating time can be especially challenging without much past experience to guide you. This is why it is crucial to track your hours, regardless whether you are working hourly or not; you need to collect data about your process to perfect these estimates.
- It can be hard to create flat rates for certain tasks, such as requests for small edits to existing designs. For example, I have a client that requires sporadic updates to her restaurant's menu throughout the year. It is hard to predict when these ad hoc needs will emerge and how many changes will be necessary, so estimating a flat fee becomes too challenging. For these types of small or unpredictable projects, I recommend charging hourly instead.
- Since working quickly is incentivized, the potential for rushing and making mistakes increases.
- If the client begins to scope creep, you need to advocate for yourself. For some, this can feel uncomfortable addressing with the client. However, if your proposal is written thoroughly, these conversations should be easier. See "Common issues with clients," in Chapter 4, for how to deal with scope creepers.
- Beware excessive revisions with flat rates; they will quickly cut into your profitability. For example, you charged a flat rate of $500 for a project because you estimated twenty hours of work. However, the client has asked for revision after revision after revision; you've now worked thirty-three hours on the project. Suddenly, your hourly rate is ~$15/hour, rather than the $50/hour you anticipated ($500/20 estimated hours vs $500/33 actual hours). This is why you must limit the number of edits that are included in your flat fee. For instance, your proposal could stipulate that the $500 flat rate includes an initial presentation of three different design options for the client to choose from, then two rounds of edits. If the client wants a third (or more) round of edits, you charge an additional fee of $50/hour. Without setting a limitation on edits like this, you're responsible for every revision the client requests until the project is complete under a flat fee pricing model.
- Some of your clients might be new to the design process, so you might have to educate the client about what constitutes an edit. This might seem silly, but I once had a client who claimed they did not realize every individual email about the design—they'd sent dozens with requests and changes—counted as an edit. They challenged the final invoice and an argument ensued. After that, I define the what, how, and when of an edit in the proposal, such as:

FIRST ROUND OF EDITS

The client must compile all their feedback about the presented designs into a single email. Once that email is received by the designer, the first round of edits will begin. If the client or designer feels a call is required to discuss the emailed feedback together, it will be scheduled as soon as possible. Otherwise, the designer will begin implementing the client's feedback into the designs.

Retainer

With this pricing model, a client most often commits to a recurring payment in exchange for a set number of hours within a time period (per week, per month, per quarter). For example, for three months, the client agrees to pay $1,000 for ten hours of design work per month. A retainer functions like a subscription to your design services.

A retainer usually provides the client a discounted rate and priority on the designer's calendar as an incentive to pre-purchase design time in bulk. For instance, your normal hourly rate is $44/hour. If your client hires you for ten hours throughout the month without a retainer agreement, the total cost to them is $440. With a retainer, you give the client a discounted rate of $40/hour because they commit to purchase ten hours per month for the next six months ($400/month, $2,400 total over six months). For most retainers, if the client does not use all their pre-purchased time within the period, they lose those hours.

Not all retainers must be based on prepaid hours; depending on your design services, there might be another type of exchange. For example, your retainer agreement might be that you create ten social media images per month for the client for a set fee. This type of retainer can help avoid some of the challenges of hourly based retainers, but it is not always an option.

Retainer advantages

- For the designer, a retainer creates stable income and steady work.
- For the client, a retainer often provides a discount on design services and prioritizes their work in the designer's queue.
- Forming a long-term relationship with a client makes working together more efficient. By becoming familiar with one another, you avoid a constant learning curve; you can get straight to work because you understand the other's business and processes.
- It reduces administrative tasks, such as writing multiple proposals or invoices, for a repeat client.

Retainer challenges

- For a potential client, a retainer can feel risky if they do not have consistent work for you, especially if they "use it or lose it" with their allotted hours.
- You're working at a discount. Having steady income over a period of time may reduce this worry, but you must ensure that your discounted rate is still profitable.
- Managing your schedule can become tricky. Since the client is pre-paying for hours, you know you need to set aside that time for them, but when? It can feel like you're on edge waiting for their requests to come in at any moment. I recommend requiring a meeting at the beginning of each retainer time period (say if it's monthly, have a one-per-month meeting) as part of the agreement. At this meeting, have the client discuss their anticipated design tasks for the time period, so you can better plan your calendar.
- With a retainer client expecting to be a priority, they can feel entitled to your time and attention. It's important that you still create boundaries with them. For instance, can a retainer client email you on a Tuesday evening and expect you to complete the ten hours' worth of work before Wednesday afternoon? In your retainer agreement, you must set expectations for project requests and turnaround times.
- Scope creep can become heightened in retainer models. For example, retainer clients might expect a long list of thirty tasks to get accomplished within a month, when only five can realistically be completed within their set number of hours. You must be good at communicating with the client about what can be accomplished within their purchased time, and if additional hours are needed, how they will be agreed on, when they will be completed, and what price they will be invoiced for.
- You also need to consider what types of tasks are included in the scope of the retainer, and how you handle requests that fall outside of that. Imagine if a client expects you to create a logo within the allotted ten hours for their monthly $400 retainer fee. However, you know a logo should take thirty-five hours to complete, and you normally charge a flat rate of $2,000 for that service. If your retainer does not outline that logos are not part of the deal, you risk losing money on a type of work that is normally more profitable.
- Like the phrase, "putting all your eggs in one basket," you can become overly dependent on retainer clients because of their perceived stability. If they decide to not renew their retainer, how would that impact your freelancing business and your financial picture? It's a good idea to keep a diverse client roster—some on retainer and some that are not.

Other pricing considerations

Not every client needs to be charged equally

Designers rarely have a set menu of prices. Instead, you must consider various factors to determine how much to charge above your baseline profitable rate for a project, such as:

- ***The size of the potential client.*** If you're proposing to do work for a global corporation, you'll likely charge them more than a small local business. This is because your work for the global corporation has an increased market value; their larger budgets, multinational reach, and profit they stand to make off of your work is much different than the mom-and-pop shop down the street.
- ***How busy you are.*** If you are in a slow freelancing season without much design work, you may propose a lower price—closer to your baseline profitable cost—in hopes the potential client will be more likely to hire you. If you are having a very busy freelancing season, you may propose a much higher price point; you're less worried about acquiring this project because your calendar is already packed. However, if you do land the project, you want to make the late nights and weekends that will be required to fit it in worth your time.
- ***How demanding the client will be.*** Some clients are more challenging and needier than others, and you should be compensated for the additional time and energy they require. For example, if the client seems indecisive, wants to meet outside of your normal working hours, or has a difficult personality to work with, you should up your price.

A project can use multiple pricing models

For most design projects, there are multiple components (phases and/or deliverables). If parts of a project can be assigned a flat rate, do so; as you've learned, this model will likely be more appealing to a potential client, and you have more earning potential. For everything else, an hourly model or retainer will likely make more sense. For instance, imagine you're developing a proposal to design a website, then maintain the site for the client after it's live. The client has less clarity about their needs in the maintenance phase, but they "know there will be menu updates, event listings, and photo swaps needed throughout the year." The design phase of the project will be predictable and controllable—you have a clear design process for websites that allows you to set limitations and estimate labor time—that makes a flat fee the best choice. However, the maintenance phase is better suited for an hourly rate because the work is unpredictable; you cannot anticipate what the updates will entail yet, so it's better to go with the less risky pricing model. Later on, if you've maintained the site for a while and a predictable pattern emerges, you can suggest a new proposal and a different pricing model to the client.

Educate the client on how to get the most for their money

Many times, a potential client needs and wants more design than they can afford with their budget. It will be your job as the designer to propose where to allocate their money to get the most bang for their buck. It's not uncommon to include a few different options in a proposal, at different price points, to give the potential client choices. This gives them agency, but also serves as a tool to educate them about the cost and value of design.

Often working with smaller companies such as mom-and-pops, design studio Matey (interview, page 50) has had to "educate, educate, educate" when developing pricing structures for clients. Matey said that many potential clients approach them with one-off needs such as a T-shirt graphic, postcard, or even a logo, which are not the best investments for small businesses:

> *We want our clients, especially those with tighter budgets, to get the most value for their money. If we only make a single T-shirt design, we have to charge a higher hourly rate or flat fee that makes the small job worth our time; as a team of two, our time is a very finite resource. Once you combine our invoice for the T-shirt design with what they pay to have shirts produced, they rarely sell enough to make their money back.*

Instead, Matey's team talks through why investing in a larger brand package—where those swag-type items can be rolled in—while more expensive up-front, will create a better long-term return for the client's business, rather than only making a single T-shirt design for them.

Leave a little room for negotiation

If a client wants to negotiate the price, you must have room to come down and still be profitable.

Pricing also includes your overhead expenses

Overhead expenses are the costs you have that are not tied directly to a specific project or client. Anything that you require to freelance generally, such as your laptop, design software, supplies, and an office space, would be considered an overhead. If your freelancing business grows and you incur more overhead expenses, you will need to revisit your pricing to account for your additional expenses.

Don't forget taxes

Taxes impact your profitability; you might think you are making $1,000 on a project, when in reality if you pay a 25 percent tax rate, you are only really taking home $750. Tax rates and rules vary based on where you live; conduct research, connect with your local business organizations and resources, and/or work with an accountant to ensure you're properly following tax regulations. If you are required to pay taxes, set aside a portion of each project's profits to account for them; this way, you will have the ability to pay your bill when it's due.

As you gain experience, your prices should go up

If you work a full-time job, you likely receive raises based on the amount of time you've been at the company or by adding new skills to your resume; this should be the same with your freelancing. Most designers raise their rates incrementally every year. If you decide to do this, let existing clients know in advance (usually a few months before) that their prices will increase, and how that will impact them (sometimes existing clients receive a special deal or different options). If you lose clients when you raise your rates, try to be optimistic—you're making space for folks who value you and your services.

Stay up to date with market trends and inflation

Economic fluctuations, from booms to recessions, can impact your profitability. For example, if the market trends downwards, potential clients might be more conservative or fearful with their budgets; to continue to land projects during this time, you may need to adjust your rates, payment schedules, or how you pitch the value of your services. You do not need to become an economics expert, but learning current general market trends from a reputable news source will help protect your bottom line. For instance, imagine it is reported that inflation rose by 3 percent in the last year. If you're unaware of this inflation data and do not factor it into your pricing, you're automatically taking a pay cut. However, by staying informed, you can recalibrate your rates to account for rising costs, and limit or offset potential profit losses.

Speak openly about money with your design friends

Talking about money with friends can feel taboo, but it's good to have a few local designers you feel comfortable doing this with. If I'm uncertain about pricing a project, I'll ask my friend Courtney what she'd generally charge, and vice versa. People like her help me determine the local market value for design better than any book or online resource ever could. By chatting about our rates openly, it's like an underground unionization; we all benefit if no one is deeply undercutting or outpricing the others.

Determining a payment schedule

Once you set your total price, you need to determine how you will get paid over the course of the project. You should never wait to receive payment until the completion of a project, otherwise you risk never being paid at all; a client could easily walk away with your initial ideas or finished design work without compensating you.

Instead, the client should pay you in installments throughout the project. See Figure 3.10 to learn how pricing correlates with your project timeline. This method reduces financial damage if non-payment occurs, as you are compensated for your labor along the way. For example, if you wait until the end of a project to be paid and the client disappears, you have lost 100 percent of the fee. However, if you received a few payments along the way (75 percent of the total fee), and the client refuses to pay the last installment, you're only down by 25 percent of the total fee (not great, but better than 100 percent). The installments should align with specific phases or milestones in your project timeline, rather than specific deliverables. This creates a relationship between project actions and project payment. In the event the client ghosts you or refuses to pay, there is a clear "stop gap" where you do not continue into the next phase until the issue is resolved.

The longer the project, the more installments there might be. If it's a small project, it might be only two installments, whereas a larger project might be four or more. However, the installment you must always require is the *deposit—an upfront payment of 25–50 percent of the total project estimate that commits the client and the designer to the project.* A deposit is standard design industry practice. If the

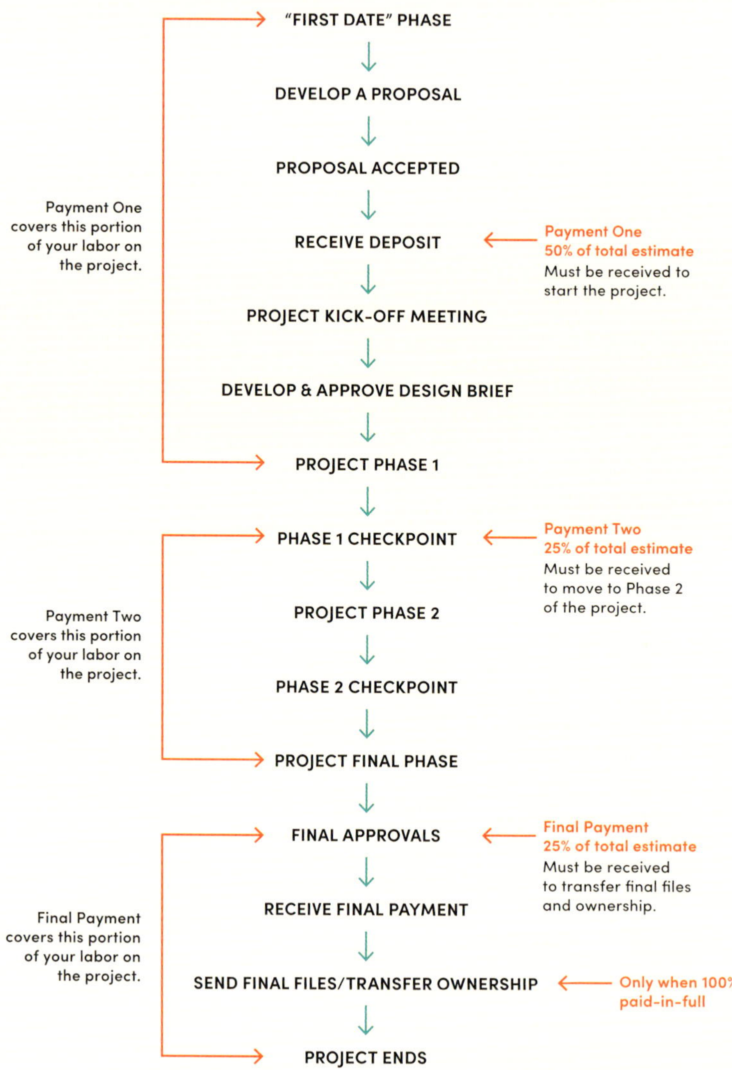

Figure 3.10 Timeline with payment schedule.

client balks at paying it, I would not work with them; it likely means they do not have the money, have no intention to pay you for your services, and/or they do not value your time.

Similarly, the last project payment is another key installment. Your proposal should state that you will turn over final high-resolution files and/or usage once the final invoice has been paid in full. While withholding these items can feel uncomfortable, it is the best way for a designer to retain agency while they await final payment. I recommend sending your last invoice slightly ahead of project completion and reminding the client of this policy along with it. This gives the client time to pay the invoice with enough time to stay on schedule and meet project deadlines. If they owe you anything to complete the work, this will hopefully hurry them along too.

Tailor your portfolio

In this section of a proposal, a link to your online portfolio will work. However, this is an opportunity to show off additional design samples that demonstrate your expertise. As you gain more experience, you will have an archive of projects that you do not show in your portfolio but that you can draw from to include in your proposals. For example, not every book I've designed is on my portfolio website. However, if I am writing a proposal for a book design project, I will go into my project archive and pull more images to include in the proposal to prove to the client that I have ample experience in that specific area. If you can tailor your project samples, especially ones that are not public on your online site, it is a pleasant surprise for the potential client to see something new. You can embed these additional samples right in the proposal itself, or you can share an unlinked, hidden, and/or password-protected page on your portfolio site that features these.

That scary legal language

The last big piece of a proposal is your terms and conditions, also known as a contract, that outlines specific policies you have if the prospective client decides to work with you. Your location will determine certain legal clauses, as different governments have varying laws related to things such as copyright and intellectual property (IP) that affect designers. Look to professional design organizations in your country to see if they have advice on or templates for legal language. In the United States, the AIGA (American Institute of Graphic Arts)—the professional association for design—has great contract examples, while books such as *Graphic Artists Guild Handbook, 16th Edition: Pricing & Ethical Guidelines* by the Graphic Artists Guild includes contract templates. While it is tempting, do not copy and paste legal clauses from the internet or another source if you do not understand the language. Nothing is more embarrassing than a client reading through your terms and conditions and asking you what something means, and *you have no idea*. Only include what you feel confident about and are willing to enforce if there's an issue. If you're taking on an abundance of client work, a worthwhile investment is spending an hour or two with a lawyer to draw up a personalized terms and conditions document for you. In that session, they will explain each item to you, which will build your confidence about your policies.

Your terms and conditions can change over time. As you freelance more, I guarantee you will want to update your terms, especially those that help wrangle problematic clients. For instance, in Unsold Studio's contract, we initially did not include a late fee if a client missed an invoice. However, after a client failed to pay us for months and it took a lot of energy chasing them, you bet we included it after that. Below, I've outlined a few of the policies I learned to add after issues arose in my own practice:

- ***A proposal expiration date.*** What happens if you write a proposal, and the person ghosts you for a year? Then they come back and expect you to fulfill the proposal you wrote 365 days ago? In a year, you might have raised your prices or your calendar now cannot accommodate their project. Unsold Studio proposals are valid for thirty days. This means if the person comes back to us after thirty-one days, we have the ability to edit the proposal or to turn the project down. Most of the time, we still honor the proposals, but we feel better knowing we have the option to make changes or opt-out if needed.
- ***Hours of operation/availability.*** In my experience working as a freelancer, some clients think you live at your desk all day and night, and are on-call for them. If you want to run your business this way, that's your call, but I began including my availability in my terms and conditions. I outline that I work Monday through Friday, 9:00 a.m. to 5:00 p.m. This way, if a client emails me on a Saturday morning asking for a last-minute edit, I'm not obligated to respond. I can if I want to, but I can also enjoy my weekends too.
- ***Project expenses.*** Certain projects require you to purchase specific materials or rent equipment, but who is responsible for paying those costs? Some expenses you may choose to fold into your overall project cost, while others you might tag on to the client's final invoice. Your terms and conditions should outline what additional expenses the client will incur, and the process for them to approve these purchases and be billed for them. For instance, with my clients, typefaces can be an unexpected expense—many non-designers do not realize a license is required to use certain font families. I list typeface licensing under potential project expenses in my terms, but I also make sure to educate the client about said expense. Throughout the project, I provide the client a selection of typefaces at different price ranges and receive a final approval before making any purchases. This way, there are no unexpected surprises when I attach a receipt (keep a copy of those) and expect reimbursement at the end of the project.
- ***Payment terms and late fees.*** When you receive a bill from the water or electric company, they are not due instantly; there is a certain amount of time to pay until it is considered late. Similarly, you need to set your policy on how long the client has to settle the invoice. Most folks will include a "net #," which means how many days after the invoice is dated that it is due. For example, "Net 7" means within seven days, "Net 15" means within fifteen days, and

"Net 30" means within thirty days. If the client misses the payment deadline, include what the ramifications are, such as a late fee. Some late fees charge a certain percent of the invoice, and it accrues until the bill is paid in full. Most importantly, be sure to add the methods of payment you accept, so the client knows how they can square up with you when an invoice does arrive.

- ***Rush fees.*** What happens if the client wants something fast? Many full-time jobs pay "time and a half" or "overtime pay" if you work extra hours—a rush fee can work like this for freelancers. If you're going to be working longer hours to meet a quick deadline for a client, you should earn more money. You need to outline what "fast" means—do you charge a rush fee if the client requests something to happen within forty-eight hours, a week, two weeks, over a weekend? Be clear about what constitutes a "rush" and what the fee is.
- ***Ownership and licensing of work.*** This topic can get complicated quickly, but essentially it should describe how and when the client and the designer can use the work that was created. Different design projects have different licensing and ownership considerations. For example, for a video project, you and the client agree that the clip can be shown online in the United States market for the next six months. However, if they decide they want to expand their reach to the Canadian market, they would need to ask your permission. At that point, you could ask for an additional licensing fee, as the client will likely increase their profits from the larger target audience. Similarly, with illustrations, you might license a drawing to be used in a specific issue of a magazine at 3" x 3". Then, if you see the client using the image another way, say on a T-shirt they are selling online, you would have legal recourse to stop this new usage and gain a portion of proceeds from the T-shirt sales. With branding projects, I normally hand off the ownership rights to the client upon their final payment, but I retain promotional rights. The client I design for should own their logo—not me. However, I want to retain the promotional rights so I can show the work in my portfolio and submit for design awards to attract more clients. If the client disagrees to you sharing the work publicly—say they request you sign an NDA (non-disclosure agreement)—you should increase your total fee because you will not be able to benefit from promoting the project.
- ***Cancellation.*** What happens if you or the client wants to end the project before it is completed? The cancellation clause should include how you initiate the breakup such as the amount of notice you must give one another if you want to break up. This is similar to how many full-time jobs require you to give two weeks' notice before officially quitting. It should also address any outstanding payments; many terminations require the client to pay for work created up until that point in the project. If any work has been produced prior to the cancellation, it should outline who owns said work.
- ***Catastrophic events.*** The unexpected could happen—an extreme weather event, a political crisis, or a health issue—that makes delivering the work on-time difficult or impossible. If something out of your control happens like this, are you or the client liable—could either sue the other for breaking the contract? Designer Aaliyah Moore (interview, page 143) said she includes a policy about catastrophic events in her terms and conditions, as she worries

how our climate crisis will impact her work. "With more extreme weather events happening, what happens if the electricity or internet goes down during a powerful storm? I want to ensure I will not be held responsible in case I'm affected and cannot fulfil my duties to the client."

Some terms and conditions include a *"force majeure" clause, which is a French term that translates as "superior force,"*[1] *which absolves liability in the event of reasons beyond your control.* OuterEdit team members Ryan and Shermeen Tan (interview, page 107) said they learned the benefits and risks of this clause during the COVID-19 pandemic. They worked with a large company who wanted to use their contract instead of OuterEdit's, which is a normal occurrence when working with bigger clients. In that company's version of terms, their cancellation clause included force majeure. After OuterEdit survived the COVID-19 pandemic, which Ryan says is his most memorable moment because they committed themselves to prioritizing the jobs and livelihoods of their team through that time, it was important to ensure a pandemic was not included under the force majeure umbrella. Further outbreaks and lockdowns were still very much a possibility at that time, and OuterEdit wanted to ensure the bigger company could not easily pull out of the project due to the pandemic, leaving their team without billable work. They negotiated with the client to include separate clauses to help the interests of both parties should there have been any movement restrictions or lockdowns imposed due to COVID-19 or any future pandemics.

- ***Signature page.*** At the very end of the terms and conditions, include a place for both you and the client to sign and date the document. This demonstrates you're both in agreement about the outlined policies, making it officially legal, and you can enforce the proposal and its contents moving forward.

Interview

OuterEdit

OuterEdit is a creative agency based in Singapore that helps brands "Make Meaningful Matter." Shermeen Tan, director, and Ryan Tan, founder and executive creative director, lead the boutique studio that started as an online T-shirt shop. Their team and projects have scaled up over the years, gaining attention beyond their island in Southeast Asia, but this growth came from believing and investing in their local community.

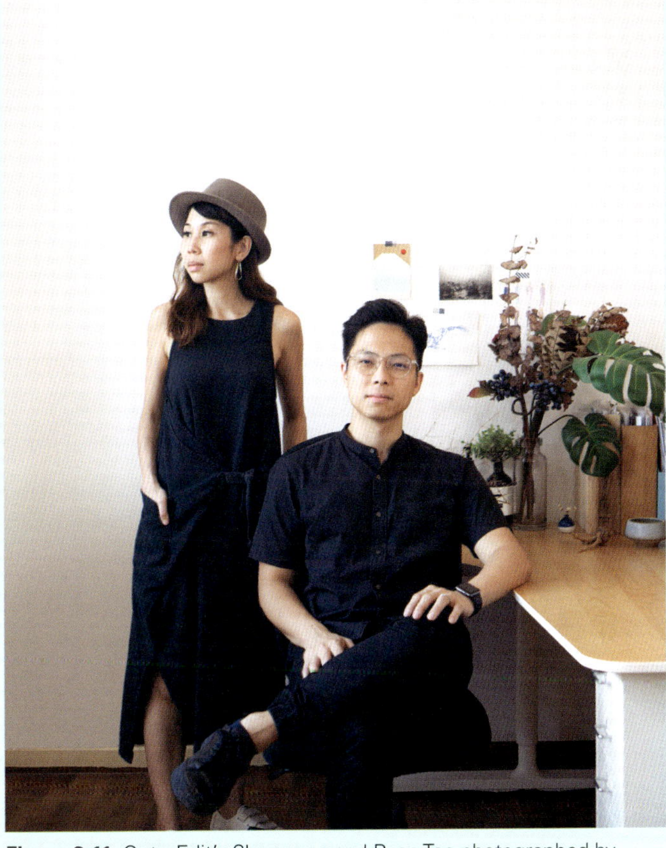

Figure 3.11 OuterEdit's Shermeen and Ryan Tan photographed by Jovian Lim.

I was lucky enough to experience their work, *Street of Clans*, in 2019, while attending Singapore Design Week. The event was a collaboration between their team and their neighbors, clan associations, on Bukit Pasoh Road, where their office is located. Bukit Pasoh Road was previously known as the "street of clans" for what was then a rich concentration of clan associations located along this road. The clan houses are usually private spaces that historically helped immigrants adapt to life in Singapore, and these communities helped shape modern Singapore by contributing to the development of the country's education, culture, and healthcare sectors. OuterEdit worked with their leaders to design an event where the clans welcomed visitors to uncover and celebrate their history and culture. With this self-initiated project, OuterEdit aimed to "tell stories of Bukit Pasoh Road in fresh, inclusive, and unexpected ways" and connect the clans with a new generation.

The brand identity and event design provided them a stunning portfolio piece, but more importantly, created long-lasting connections for their community. For me, this project served as a reminder you have agency as a designer—you do not have to wait for a potential client to start making design work. You can begin a new project by literally knocking on your neighbor's door, just like Shermeen and Ryan did to initiate *Street of Clans*.

Add your voice and vision

Singapore is a relatively new country that gained her independence in 1965. Ryan explained that design has played a crucial role in her infancy, growth, and development:

> **I believe the Singapore story is also a wonderful design story. The original Singapore designers may not have fully associated with the designations or roles of modern-day designers, but if you look back into the archives, you see our country needed to come up with design solutions to address some serious challenges when it became its own nation, from having little or no natural resources of its own, to navigating public housing, education, healthcare, and infrastructure—the list goes on. Against all odds, these solutions, and our forefathers who spearheaded them, took us from the third world to the first, mud flats to a metropolis. These solutions didn't pop out of nowhere; they had to be imagined, refined, tested, and boldly executed. We stay inspired knowing we come from that creative lineage.**

His pride for Singapore's design culture stems from his architect father, who passed away in 2010. "My father was so passionate about the local creative industry. After he died, I felt I needed to extend his legacy, and one good way to do that was to start a company that would share in his excitement and values of designing for change and good." In 2011, Ryan launched an innovative online T-shirt company that allowed for creatives from around the globe to share files and design together, overcoming language barriers, time zones, and cultural differences to collaborate. "We didn't just want it to be about a product. While the apparel side of things ended up not being our future, our process and approach to creativity and collaboration from it has served as the foundation of our design and branding work that we do up till today."

As the T-shirt work began to dissipate, OuterEdit's focus shifted to graphic design and branding work. Shermeen came on to help Ryan with his growing list of freelance design projects. "He needed some help, and then basically after that, I never left." She had attended business school, interned and worked at local agencies, and received a design diploma prior to working at OuterEdit.

The couple (yes, they're married!) are shaping Singapore's design today through their work at OuterEdit. "A lot of people look to other places like Tokyo or London to determine what should be done creatively in Singapore, but we as Singaporeans should add our voices to its design culture." Their portfolio highlights their dedication to their community, from working with local second-generation owned restaurant groups such as Song Fa Bak Kut Teh, to creating site-specific experiences for the Singapore Grand Prix, and positioning the city-state as a "leading Urban Wellness Haven" through the design of the Wellness Festival Singapore brand. Their work for these local clients has garnered international recognition. For instance, their *Good Intentions Calendar* for

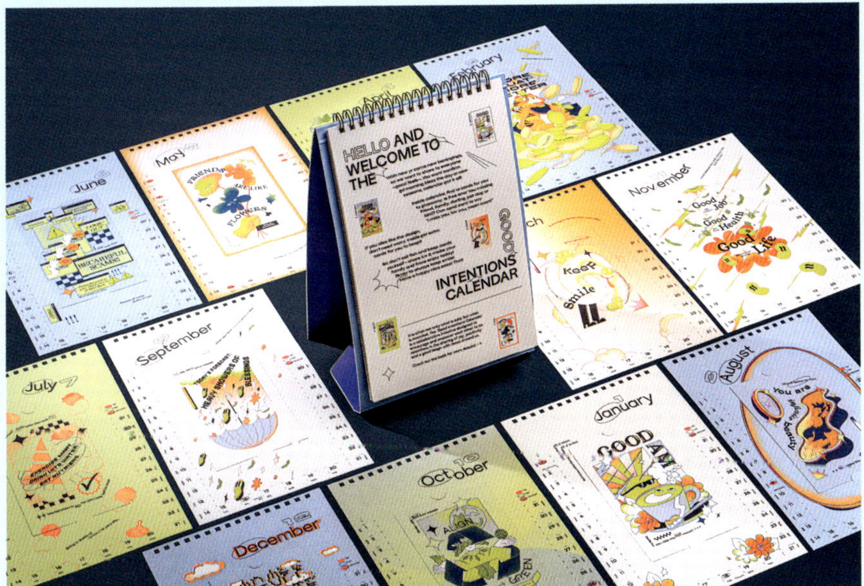

Figure 3.12 Beyond a simple print calendar, OuterEdit aspired to uplift the hearts and minds of all who received the calendar. Starting off with a shortlist of witty, well-intended wisdoms, each greeting was then paired with a custom illustration, with little Easter eggs hidden within each page. Photography by The Gentle Studio.

Singapore-based RJ Paper Pte Ltd. was long-listed for the Dezeen Awards 2022 and won the UK-based Design Week Awards 2022 in Print Communications.

Take every opportunity seriously

Early in Shermeen's freelancing career prior to collaborating with Ryan, a friend hired her to rebrand her father's thirtyish-year-old scaffolding company. While the industry wasn't one that she was familiar with, she was determined to get the project right. She went to the facility to better understand the business, then designed a brand identity and website that looked more modern and professional. Shortly after, the newly branded business caught the attention of a Japanese company, which later decided to acquire them. This was a success story for the scaffolding company, who were grateful for the new rebrand contributing to making this achievement happen.

Years later while working at OuterEdit, their team was commissioned to design a huge pavilion for the Singapore-based shopping mall Millenia Walk (MW). "The lines between creative disciplines are blurring. You have graphic designers creating physical installations. You have architects doing branding work. It's been an interesting journey to not constrain ourselves and our creativity." Shermeen encourages new freelancers to believe in "punching above your own weight because you're able to do a lot more than you imagine," and "to not be afraid to ask for help from others."

She took her own advice when there was a question about how to actually construct the pavilion, *MW Happy Park*. She returned to her scaffolding client to ask for advice and a favor. They agreed to help, a great reminder to treat every client with care. Even though the company normally only worked on large industrial-scale projects, they sent their team to build the innovative structure. For Shermeen, that project was "such a cool, full circle moment—from doing their branding project as a young, budding designer to years down the road, to seeing our teammates and client work with them to create something bigger than I could have imagined."

Find ways to be creative in non-creative environments

Before founding OuterEdit, Ryan worked in other roles outside of the design field. His initial interest in a creative career started in high school, where his coursework centered around design. However, after graduation he served in the National Service in Singapore. Even in the regimented army and police force, he found ways to express his creativity:

> **I found myself in a traditionally non-creative environment, but the thing is that creative challenges abound, everywhere. While new ways of seeing and thinking may not always be appreciated in every situation, I often couldn't help but to contribute ideas that other people in the service wouldn't necessarily have thought of. It trained me for my ideas with people of different professions, backgrounds and perspectives.**

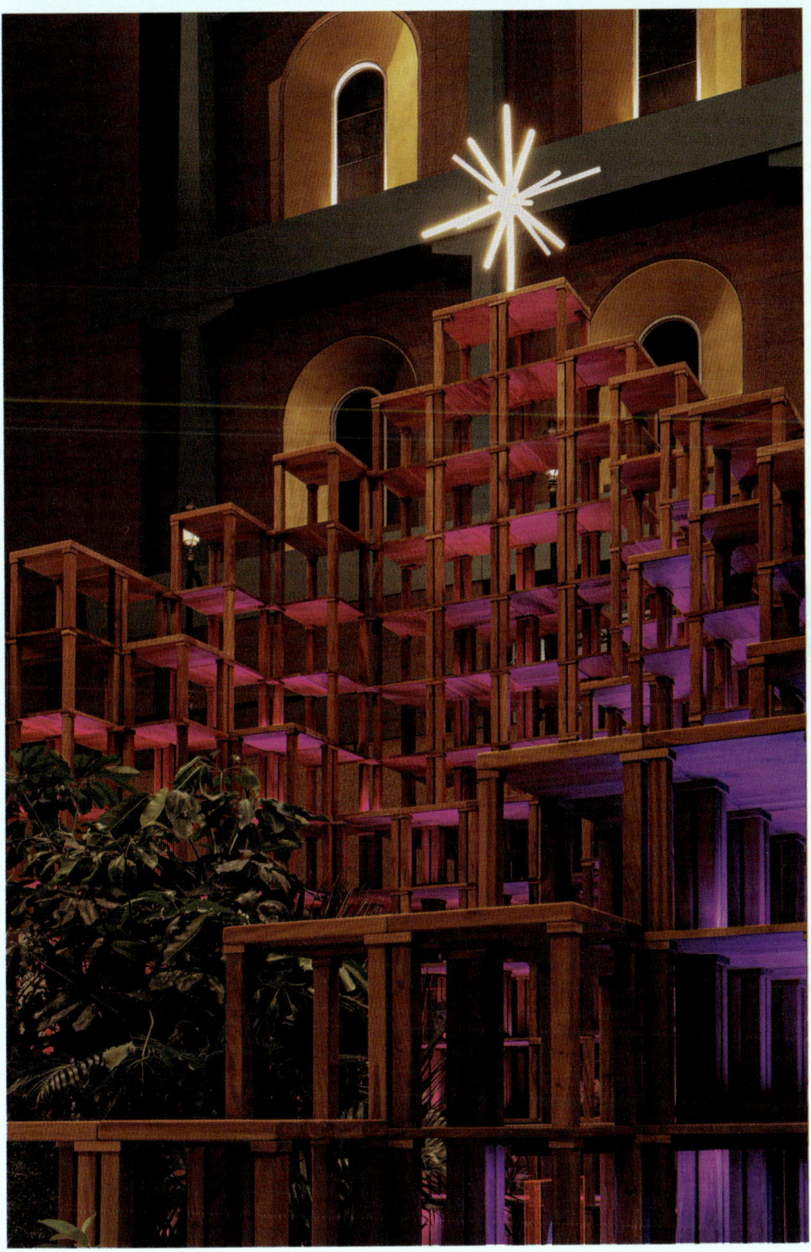

Figure 3.13 Due to Singapore's limited access to natural resources, imported fir trees and artificial decorative structures are commonly used to usher in the holidays. After Christmas, these usually end up in landfills, creating unnecessary waste and harm to the environment. OuterEdit designed their tree for Millenia Walk to empower local communities, and to give a second and third life to solid wood salvaged from fallen local trees. Photography by Nic Loh.

After his service, Ryan pursued business school. To fulfill his need for creativity, he used his Photoshop skills to start freelancing outside of class time. "I'm fully self-taught. I didn't go through design school, but I learnt by reverse engineering artwork that I'd find on free postcards and public posters that I was drawn to. To gain as much market experience as I could, I took on small gigs designing menus, tickets, cards, and invites for cafes, bars, clubs, and restaurants around Nottingham." He laughed looking back on how inefficiently he'd used the tools to create this work. Upon graduation, he was hired by the Singapore Tourism Board, which would later become one of OuterEdit's clients. He worked there for three and a half years, working on projects such as the inaugural Formula 1 Singapore Grand Prix and the Singapore Pavilion at the 2010 World Expo in Shanghai, before leaving to start a company.

Ryan's story is a good reminder that a design career does not have to follow a linear path and not every wonderful design outcome is "going to come through the figurative front door; sometimes you will come to things from a different entry point—like the back door or a cat flap." Shermeen advises,

> **It's alright to have a destination in mind for your career, but hold it loosely to guide you. Sometimes when the plan's too rigid, you may always feel like you're failing along the way and become demoralized if things don't go perfectly. Instead—especially in the first few years—try things out, experiment, and put yourself out there. All of that will help shape you and the type of work you want to do later on. Don't be scared if the destination changes along the way.**

Equalize power

On their journey, Ryan and Shermeen learned having balance with their clients is key to running a successful project. This balance can come in the form of a good set of terms and conditions, where both you and your client feel equally protected before starting design. They recommended that if you're freelancing regularly, an important early investment is to hire a lawyer to perfect the language and to teach you the meaning of terminology in the document.

One part of an agreement that many freelancers miss is the right to retain their intellectual property, especially for the ideas the client does not choose during the design process. "You should be able to retain ownership over the ideas the client does not select. You should be able to repurpose your own ideas and to even share the 'unsuccessful' ones with others or as part of your portfolio."

Shermeen and Ryan add,

It's also important to find yourself, your approach, and style of work, and use that as a north star to guide you across all companies and clients. Without much experience, it's easy to let larger clients direct you and your design process because that's the natural power dynamic: you're an individual or small team, and they're bigger and established. With small clients, like neighborhood businesses, you're on more equal ground. This allows you to collaborate more easily with one another with a more balanced power dynamic.

They continue, "However, what's most important is the mutual respect in the relationship, and a spirit of collaborative openness, honesty, transparency, fairness, and their willingness to see you as a true creative partner. This can be found in the best sorts of clients, whether they be small or large businesses."

Leave your community better than you found it

Ryan and Shermeen feel a sense of duty when it comes to using their design skills. "We have creative abilities, and we also have an obligation to do the best we can within the communities we're in. Design isn't just a business or an industry—it's a social thing. For us, it's a responsibility to leave the community in a better place than we first found it." They believe that design is a people-centered business. "If you take care of your people—from clients, colleagues to partners and your community—your work will reflect that positivity. We believe it's more sustainable long-term in your career to focus on that than chasing the brands, the money, a busy project calendar, and so on."

The duo has set a goal for OuterEdit to "become one of the most progressive creative businesses in Singapore." To fulfill this, they're enacting forward-thinking policies for their in-house team, but also advocating for industry change outside their office walls. They worked pro bono on the project *Don't Mind If I Ask*, an industry survey about Singapore's communications design industry, with other volunteers over three years. The project was made "with the hope of encouraging all industry stakeholders to better understand, value and progress the local creative industry that each stakeholder works with and within." By taking on this additional—often hard—work, Ryan, Shermeen, and their teammates are proving they don't just talk about improving their communities—they're taking action and following through.

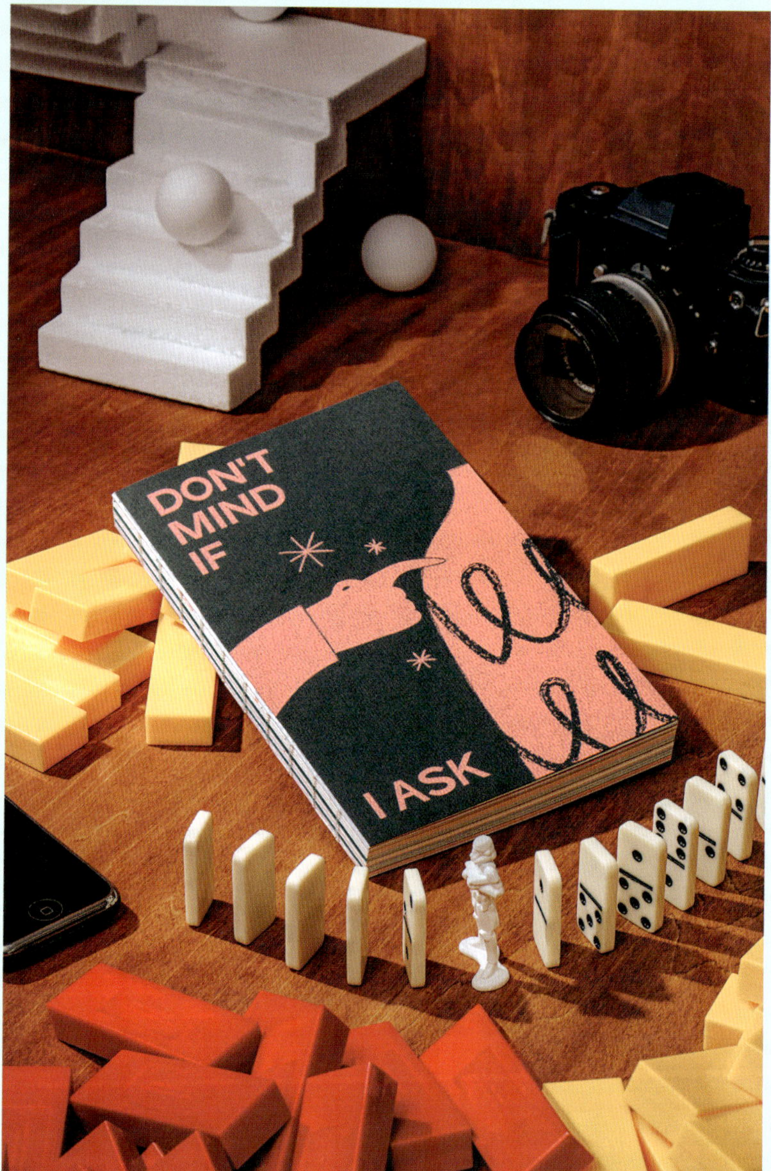

Figure 3.14 Published in 2022 after three years of development, *Don't Mind If I Ask* is an independent inquiry on the wellbeing of Singapore's communications design industry organized from the ground-up for and by the community by industry volunteers. Photography by The Gentle Studio.

To learn more about Shermeen, Ryan, and OuterEdit.

outeredit.com
@outeredit

Sending a proposal

Review the proposal. Turn on spell check. Ask a friend to look it over, especially the first few. Then send it off to the client with a reminder of the proposal's expiration date, cross your fingers, and hope they accept!

The waiting game

Many potential clients communicate that they are in a rush to have their project completed, but when it comes time to review your proposal, their pace suddenly slows. This may be because:

- they solicited proposals from multiple designers. The potential client will want to receive information from all prospective collaborators before making their final selection.
- they have multiple decision-makers who need to read through your proposal before signing off. This is why it is important to ask about who the project decision-makers are in the "first date" phase; the more hands your proposal must go through before being accepted (or rejected), the longer you should expect to wait on a decision.
- they are carefully reviewing your proposal, and potentially preparing questions or a counteroffer.
- their project timeline is not as "rushed" as they claimed.

In my experience, you will usually hear something back from the potential client within a week; this may simply be confirmation they've received your proposal, a list of questions, or their final decision. If I have not heard back within one week, I recommend following up with the potential client. In these situations, I write something like:

> *Hi (insert potential client name),*
>
> *I'm reaching out to see if you have any questions or concerns about the proposal I sent last week. If so, I'm happy to schedule a time in the next few days for us to chat through and finesse the project details.*
> *Thanks again for the consideration of my proposal, and looking forward to hearing from you.*
>
> *Best,*
> *Meaghan*

This type of reminder usually will prompt a response. If not, I will send along a final reminder a few days before the proposal's expiration date, such as:

> *Hi (insert potential client name),*
>
> *I'm sending along a friendly reminder that the proposal I sent a few weeks ago for your project is set to expire on (insert date). In order to schedule your*

project on my calendar and meet your project deadline, I'll need to receive the approval and signed proposal by that date. Let me know if you have any questions or concerns. Hope all is well!

Best,
Meaghan

If you do not hear back after the second reminder, you likely never will. This unfortunately happens on occasion, and it is why the proposal expiration date is helpful; it provides a set time for you to move on from the opportunity if the potential client takes no action.

As an eternal optimist, I reframe this frustrating situation by reminding myself I likely just avoided a problematic client; their lack of communication skills would have negatively impacted the project if we moved forward, when more of my time, money, and energy was invested. This scenario reiterates why it's vital to be efficient in the "first date" and proposal writing phases; there is no guarantee you will land a project (or receive an official rejection from a potential client). Return to Chapter 1, "If you need to find a freelance project," if a potential client ghosted you after you sent a proposal (I told you this was kind of like dating).

If they approve the proposal

Congrats! You landed a project!

The next steps include:

- ***Signing the proposal.*** Make sure both parties (you and the client) have signed and dated the agreement, and you both have a copy for your records.
- ***Send an invoice for the project deposit.*** See Figure 3.15 to learn about elements to include in an invoice. At Unsold Studio, we use an online accounting service, Freshbooks, that includes an easy-to-use invoicing tool. It's helpful because it shows us when the client has viewed the invoice (so no one can say they never received it) and allows payments through their portal. Until you are ready to invest in something like that, you can simply attach an invoice to an email.
- ***Schedule a project kick-off meeting.*** If you were efficient with your "first date" phase, you most likely have the essential information about the project. However, there is likely more information you need to gather from the client now that you're officially invested in the project. A kick-off meeting gives you the opportunity to ask more questions and dig deeper into the details before you begin the design phase. I recommend developing another template with these more detailed questions. Send these ahead of the meeting to give the client a chance to form their thoughts. Sometimes, the answers you receive may feel redundant from the "first date" phase—that's actually great. Hearing the information repeated will affirm you're on the right track. If anything new

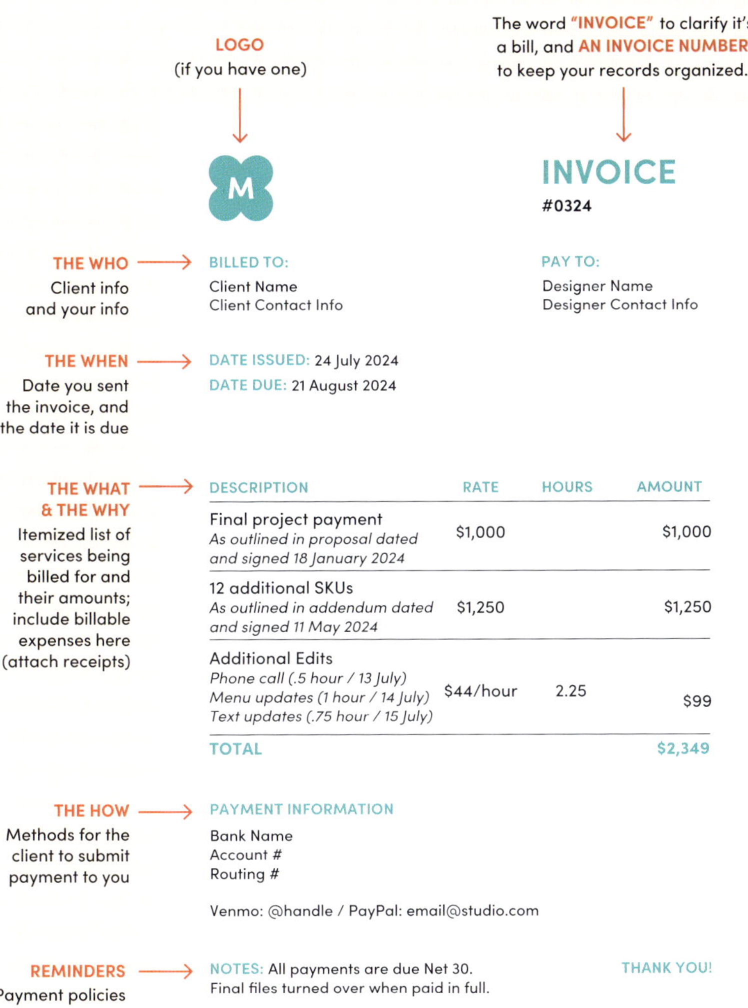

Figure 3.15 Invoice sample.

or surprising emerges, you still have the chance to "course correct" the proposal, if needed, before fully diving in.

All project decision-makers must come to this meeting. You want to hear from everyone on their team (and let them hear from you), to build consensus and avoid issues later. For instance, imagine Anna from the client's team was not a part of the "first date" phase and does not attend the project kick-off meeting because she has a very busy schedule. However, she attends the first design presentation, and her feedback completely derails your solutions. If you had heard Anna's ideas and concerns prior to designing, you would have gone in a completely different direction. While it may seem annoying or feel like you're wasting precious time, reschedule the project kick-off meeting, if needed, to ensure everyone can be present.

At the kick-off meeting, also remind the client if they have any "homework" to get the project started, such as sending you files or content you need to begin. After the kick-off meeting, I recommend developing a design brief with the information you gathered, as outlined in "Managing the project," in Chapter 4.

Now get your kick-off meeting scheduled, send a calendar invitation, as well as a meeting agenda and any other necessary materials such as questionnaires ahead of time. These actions will help the client see you as a project leader.

Move forward to Chapter 4, "Working together."

If they want to negotiate the proposal

Sometimes a potential client will accept your proposal right away, no questions asked. And sometimes, there's a negotiation that needs to happen. Most often I've found issues arise over the price or the timeline. What to do if they:

- ***Have an issue with the price.*** Hopefully you've built in some wiggle room to come down in price as mentioned in "How to price your work," earlier in this chapter. If you have, there's an ability for you to lower the project price without it being a problem for your bottom line. If you haven't, you might try the other options below:
  - Offer a different payment plan, perhaps one that has more installments. This might work better with the potential client's cash flow to pay smaller amounts more often. For example:

    Initial proposed payment plan:
    Project Total: $5,000
    Payment 1: Project Deposit: 50%—$2,500
    Payment 2: Upon Project Completion: 50%—$2,500
    New proposed payment plan:
    Project Total: $5,000
    Payment 1: Project Deposit: 30%—$1,500
    Payment 2: Upon completion of Project Phase 1: 25%—$1,250

Payment 3: Upon completion of Project Phase 2: 20%—$1,000
Payment 4: Upon completion of Project Phase 3: 15%—$750
Payment 5: Upon completion of Project Phase 4: 10%—$500

If you go down this route, your project timeline will need to be updated to align with the new payment plan; you would need more milestones along the way to ensure if the client does not make a payment, you have a "stop gap" in place.

- Revisit the question about their budget. Now that your price is in front of them, the potential client may be more willing to discuss how much they'd like to spend. If they're forthcoming about their "maximum spend" at this point, you could reconfigure the deliverables around that price point. Instead of having their whole wish list of items and features, perhaps you prioritize the three that are most important and save the rest for a future project. This will allow you to lower your price because you'll be doing less labor, which is a good compromise to make.
- Reinforce why design is a smart investment for the potential client. Many of your early clients, especially small businesses, will be working on tight budgets. It is important that you can explain to them how your services will improve their situation long-term; the "pain" of spending right now might feel great, but the repercussions of *not* pursuing the project might be more expensive later.

- ***Have an issue with the timeline.*** Explain the design process to the potential client and why you need that amount of time to do what you do. A lot of people assume designers can do a quick napkin sketch, then a few quick keystrokes on the computer, and voila!—the design emerges. We know this is not the case, so politely walk them through the what and the why behind each phase of the project, emphasizing that time is to ensure you create a great output for them.

  I advise you to not cut corners on your design process to meet the client's timeline. However, a few ways that you might be able to reduce the timeline without sacrificing the quality of your work are to:

  - Require the client to provide feedback faster. Perhaps you only give the client a day versus one week to provide you edits for the next phase. This puts the onus on the client to ensure the timeline is adhered to, rather than solely on you.
  - Reduce the number of edits, but with a caveat to the client. Perhaps your process normally includes the first round of design directions plus two edits. You could remove the last edit, so the timeline includes the first round of design directions plus one edit. Warn the client that you normally advise for that final round of edits, as you might not get it perfect without that second edit. However, they can take that risk to meet their deadline if they'd like.
  - If they cannot flex on the timeline, you could charge a higher fee—"a rush fee"—to meet their deadlines if you're willing to accommodate their needs.

If they reject the proposal

It will be okay

Have you been told "no" before? Of course, you have—we all have because rejection is normal. On the internet, I've come across the "100 No's Challenge" where the goal is literally to hear "no" 100 times in relation to your business. You take 100 actions—approach new clients, apply for funding, or whatever your goals may be—and normalize being turned down. To acquire this many rejections, you have to keep putting yourself out there. However, the perk of the challenge is that the probability is in your favor to hear a few yeses along the way too.

Try to learn why you weren't selected

If you feel comfortable, you can ask the client why you were not chosen for the project. It might be something simple, such as your fee was the highest among the designers that they received proposals from. By asking, you could receive some helpful feedback that will make you more competitive in the future; however, most often the client will give you a polite and vague response and that's that.

Another avenue that might help is following these "lost" clients and your freelancing "competition" on social media. While this might seem a little stalker-ish, at some point, one may share a celebratory post after the "lost" project wraps. From there, you can learn who the client did hire for the job and look through their online presence to size yourself up. Sometimes this will push you to improve your own materials. Other times, it will remind you that not every client and project is a good fit for you. For example, Lilian and I occasionally lose business to a local agency that is much flashier than us; they have a bigger team, fancier office, and a client list filled with name brands. While this annoys us, we've found some peace reminding ourselves that's not the kind of studio we are; if the client wants that type of team, it's better they went in another direction.

Things can change

Years ago, Unsold Studio was a finalist for a design project with a local nonprofit. After receiving our proposal and conducting an interview with us, we were ultimately not selected. While disappointed they went with a different designer, we were proud that we represented ourselves well, and moved on to other opportunities.

A year later, that client reached out to us. Turns out, the other designer they'd chosen was not a good fit for their team. Some of their complaints included that the designer missed deadlines, sent projects to print without their approval, and was hard to get hold of. They regretted not hiring us for the project, and hoped we'd be interested in working with them. Since then, they've become one of our long-term clients.

Move back to Chapter 1, "If you need to find a freelance project."

4

Working together

In this chapter, I will not focus on the actual design process—that's the part you should feel the most confident in as a designer—and is the bulk of the work here. Instead, you'll learn how to manage clients and meet them where they're at. The ultimate goal is to end the project with a client who feels positive about your experience together (and even better if it was so good, they tell their friends about you). To do this, you must deliver a great design outcome, but also a great customer experience along the way too.

Get a deposit!

I'm emphasizing this for good measure. The most common way new freelancers get burned is beginning work without receiving some form of compensation. Do not put yourself in a situation where you start working, make something lovely, hand it off to the client, then never hear from them again.

There's no need to feel guilty requesting a deposit, as it was outlined in your proposal (unless you're doing a project for trade or pro bono, which may be an exception to this rule). The client agreed to the payment schedule, so follow through on sending your first invoice.

Managing the project

Write (and follow) a design brief

After the kick-off meeting, I recommend writing a design brief. A design brief functions like your assignment sheet to follow during the project. While you do have your proposal that the client and you signed off on that contains this type of information, that document might be ten pages long, which is a lot of content to sift through. Instead, a design brief is a one- or two-page document that summarizes key elements of a project to keep you and the client on task. It also includes additional information that you gathered during the kick-off meeting that may not be contained in your initial proposal, such as target audience and desired project aesthetics. See an example in Figures 4.1 and 4.2.

Sometimes when I'm in design mode, I get so focused it's like I've gone down a rabbit hole. When I reemerge, I'm a bit dazed and begin to question if what I made is right or not. This is when I pull out the design brief and double check my work against its content. Similarly, if a client begins to get off track in their feedback or expectations about your work, you can redirect them to the design brief to realign them with the project.

Ask the client to sign-off on the design brief before you move into the next phase of the project. You want to be sure you're in agreement on the document, as you'll both reference it throughout the experience working together.

Be good at admin

This might be one of the least fun parts of freelancing, but it is critical. Throughout the project, stay on top of the administrative tasks that keep things running smoothly. Set meeting agendas. Send calendar invites. Take meeting notes. Get sign-offs from clients. Respond to emails. You'd be surprised how many folks are terrible at these tasks. One client told Lilian and me that while we are great designers, their team continues to hire us because we're organized and communicative, in other words, good at admin. There are ample project management tools, such as Trello, which can help you stay on top of tasks, especially if you have multiple client projects at the same time.

Overcommunicating is better than under-communicating

If your gut says you should check in with the client, do it. It might seem needy or annoying, but if you have questions, ask them. It's better to have clarification and avoid issues, than the opposite.

Make a mistake, own it and fix it

One time I designed a client's invitation that included the wrong date for the event. It went out to all the guests. I got a reasonably angry phone call from the client. While our terms and conditions did outline that our studio was not responsible for final proofing, and I could have thrown that back in the client's face, I didn't. Instead of rehashing how the problem happened, I instead said, "Let's focus on a solution." That simple phrase redirected the conversation somewhere productive, rather than a vent session that would wind the client up more. We quickly resolved the issue after that. The client continues to hire our studio for projects despite this incident, and I'm certain it's because of the way the situation was handled without chaos and blame.

DESIGN BRIEF EXAMPLE

PAGE ONE

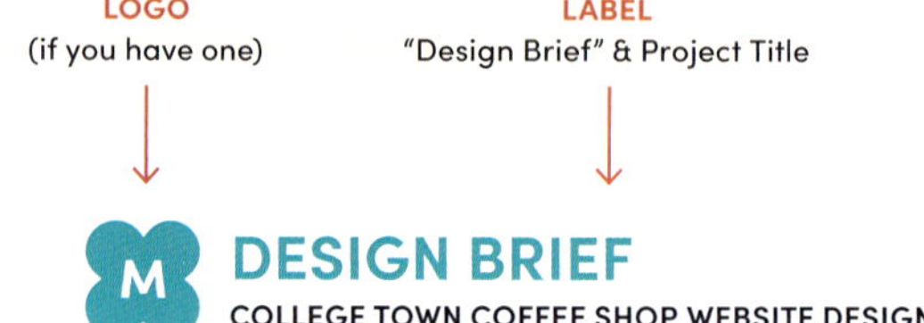

PRO TIP → Keep your information to the essentials. You still have your proposal agreement to use; the Design Brief is meant to be the high-level overview of the project details for quick reference. Bullet points and short phrases will help this be a tool that's worth using.

PROJECT DESCRIPTION

The Client wants a new website that is user-friendly, ensuring customers can easily access shop information like hours and events, and purchase products online.

ABOUT THE CLIENT

- has been locally owned and operated since 1988
- only nearby shop that offers high-quality coffee & espresso drinks late-night (open 6am–11pm daily)
- offers a community gathering space with weekly events such as acoustic music performances, club meet-ups, and classes
- in 2022, began a small product line of goods, including their coffee beans, canned cold brew, pre-packaged baked goods, and branded merchandise like reusable coffee mugs

PROJECT GOALS

- simplify site navigation (less pages) and reduce redundancies
- make site responsive and mobile-friendly
- highlight shop events and happenings
- create online shop to sell shop's product line

INFORMATION CATEGORIES → I'm using categories in this example that are commonly used in Design Briefs. However, include the type of information that best fits your unique project and client.

PROJECT AUDIENCE

- local university students (late teens, twenties)
- tech-saavy, but come to "unplug" at coffee shop (study/hang out)
- budget-conscious, but will spend on quality items

CLIENT COMPETITORS

- big national coffee chain
- cheap and fast 24-hour diner nearby

BRAND PERSONALITY

- welcoming, inclusive, and collaborative
- proud and supportive of its local community
- cares about quality, but is not snobby

1

Figure 4.1 Creative brief sample 1.

DESIGN BRIEF EXAMPLE

PAGE TWO

LIMIT PAGES →
Your Design Brief should not exceed two pages, or else it will fail to be a quick, easy tool to reference during the project. Keep it efficient!

ASSETS & DELIVERABLES

- website design
  - home page
  - seasonal menu page
  - events page
  - about page
  - contact page
  - e-commerce shop (40 product SKUs)

BUDGET

$5,000 for website build-out
~$200 per quarter for ongoing site updates and maintenance

TIMELINE

- New site must be launched by August 15, 2024 in time for when university students begin arriving back to campus for the academic year

PRO TIP →
If there are multiple decision-makers, assign one person to be the primary communicator. This will streamline how you receive information from their team, and not receive conflicting info from multiple people.

PROJECT TEAM

Kimmie, College Town Coffee Shop Owner (Decision-Maker)

Other team members to provide select content:

- Chico, Coffee Roaster: menu info and beans product info
- Val, Shop Baker: menu info and baked goods product info

APPROVALS

Kimmie is the primary decision-maker. She will be the person providing feedback and project sign-offs.

DESIGN BRIEF APPROVED BY CLIENT

SIGNATURE:
PRINT NAME / TITLE:
DATE:

DON'T FORGET TO SIGN & DATE →
This is what makes this document legal!

DESIGN BRIEF APPROVED BY DESIGNER

SIGNATURE:
PRINT NAME / TITLE:
DATE:

2

Figure 4.2 Creative brief sample 2.

Don't forget to track your time

If you're working hourly, this is a must. Follow your agreement with the client about communicating the number of hours you work. Even if you are not doing a project hourly, you need this data to better price projects in the future. By understanding your time usage, your estimations will become more accurate, and so will your prices and profitability.

Common issues with clients

You will have a difficult client—it's inevitable. Here's a few recurring archetypes:

The Scope Creeper

This client increases the project scope—accidentally, subtly, or blatantly—without offering to compensate the designer for the additional labor.

How to handle

For some small scope creeps, such as a quick text edit, you might be inclined to just do the extra task. Other times, the scope creep will be more problematic and must be addressed so you are not taken advantage of. In these instances, stay positive in your response to the client, while pointing back to the proposal and outlining next steps for the increases. For example: "Your idea for (insert increase) is great and I'd love to get that done for you. Since it was not included in our initial proposal, I will send along an addendum with updated pricing and timeline for you to sign before we start on it."

The Ghost

This client disappears and then will pop back up at the most inconvenient time, usually acting as though they never left.

How to handle

When the client finally reappears, provide them with an updated timeline. If they balk at their deadline being pushed back, refer to your policies related to client responsibilities. For example: "In order to stay on our proposed timeline, our agreement states feedback must be received from you within one week. Since this deadline was missed, the time I set aside for completing the edits has passed. If you want to pay a rush fee, I can prioritize your project in my queue. Otherwise, I will do my best to fit it in around my other current client work."

The Micromanager

This client hovers over your shoulder throughout the process and lacks trust in your decision-making.

How to handle

For these clients, use predetermined meeting points, such as kick-off meetings, design presentations, and feedback calls, to corral them. For example: "I appreciate your enthusiasm and wanting to be so involved in the process. Let's plan to discuss everything at once in our upcoming Phase Three meeting. As outlined in our proposal, this will be where I present design updates to you. It will be most productive and efficient to talk through your ideas at that checkpoint."

The Flip-Flopper

This client changes their mind, then changes it again, then wants to go back to what you had, then makes just one more change (maybe).

How to handle

Hopefully you're either charging this client hourly or you've limited their edits with a flat fee. If not—better luck next time. If you're charging hourly, an update on the time and money they've spent so far on the item in question might speed up their decision-making. If you're charging a flat fee with limited revisions, remind them how many more edits are included based on the proposal, and beyond those, additional fees will incur.

You'll notice a pattern in the responses to these difficult clients: a reliance on the proposal agreement to justify additional costs and set boundaries. While the proposal is not the be-all and end-all to ensure "good" client behavior, the outline and agreement of processes and policies at the outset of a project serve as precautionary measures. If challenging situations do arise, an effective proposal provides a road map for how to proceed. If you run into a new type of difficult client, update your proposals with clarified language or additional terms to hopefully avoid similar issues on future projects. Head to Chapter 3, "If you want to pursue the project," to guide your proposal refinement.

Setting clients up for success

If you're following my advice, some of your first clients will be small-scale; individuals, mom-and-pop businesses, and local nonprofits. These types of clients have unique needs because:

- ***Most small-scale clients do not have an in-house design team.*** This is why they are hiring you! These clients often do not have a dedicated employee overseeing their day-to-day design needs. Their teams usually run lean, and as mentioned earlier, design can be perceived as an extra rather than a necessity. While you're working with them, they have access to a designer, but when your engagement ends with them, they go back to not having a dedicated expert. Without regular contact to a designer such as an in-house design team provides, these clients might be less exposed to the process, lingo, and value of design and require more education and guidance along the way.

- ***Many small-scale clients do not have access to industry-standard design tools.*** A common complaint I've heard from small-scale clients is that designers have left them with great, but unusable work. These clients rarely license programs such as Adobe Creative Suite; some do not know what these programs are, others do not know how to use them, and some cannot afford them. Designers often forget this reality, and leave folks with solutions and file types that require design tools and skills the client does not have. This renders the client's investment in design ineffectual because they cannot implement it on their own—remember, they likely do not have an in-house designer and cannot afford to pay a freelancer for every need that arises.
- ***Many small-scale clients must be budget-conscious and value-driven.*** According to the US Chamber of Commerce in December 2023, inflation, revenue, rising interest rates, and worker shortages topped the concerns of small businesses.[1] With all of these pressures, small businesses have to be financially savvy to stay profitable.

To provide the best service to these clients, you should consider:

- ***The ease-of-implementation of your design solutions.*** Your small-scale clients will already be juggling lots of responsibilities running their business (like you), so adding design tasks—especially complicated or time-consuming ones—will overwhelm them or quickly fall to the bottom of their to-do list. However, some of these clients will want to implement design elements on their own as a way to save costs by not consistently hiring a designer. For example, I had a client who wanted a series of branded social media templates that they could use to create new content themselves. My first instinct was to design these templates in a program such as Adobe Illustrator or Photoshop—however, I knew the client did not know how to use the software and had no interest in learning. Instead, I imported design elements into the online program Canva, which is user-friendly for non-designers. I also provided the client with a tutorial as part of the scope of work. This solution required a few extra steps on my part, but ensured the client's needs were best met. Whatever you create for your client, make sure they leave the project feeling empowered and prepared to continue on their own if needed.
- ***The cost-effectiveness of your design solutions.*** As you're brainstorming ideas, you must be aware of the cost to produce them. While the proposed solution might be amazing, the reality of its expense may rule it out. For example, typeface licensing can add an additional cost to the client in a branding project. You might love the way the medium weight italic font looks in the logo design, but if the client cannot afford the $250 price tag to legally use it, it's ultimately not an option. As you're designing, the cost for the client has to be on your mind—it would be cruel to present something they fall in love with that you know they cannot financially commit to. If you're unsure of their budget for production costs, especially if they were not a part of your proposal, present and discuss solutions that have a range of price points.
- ***Creating a network with them.*** With some clients being unfamiliar with the

design world, you serve as their gateway to it. Help your client connect with other resources—creatives, vendors, and tools—that they need along the way. Our studio often recommends our go-to social media manager, photographer, web developer, and printer friends to our small business clients. These recommendations are appreciated by all, and it means we frequently share clients and collaborate with folks we love to work with. And be open to references from your client—who knows what great people you'll meet through them.

Presenting your work

Start with directions

For many of your clients, this will be the first time they're going through the design process. They might feel uncomfortable or unsure of what their role is in the process. Before every presentation, give the client clear guidance about what will happen. You could say something like:

> *I'm going to share three different directions that are possible solutions for the project. As I present, you are welcome to ask questions or give immediate feedback if you have any. There's no pressure to make any decisions now. I will send the slide deck after the meeting concludes and encourage you to review and sleep on it before sending me feedback. As a reminder, I'll want to receive feedback within one week via email or in a scheduled meeting. Any questions before we kick off the presentation?*

This will ease their concerns, focus them on their role in the meeting, and it will also position you as the leader of the meeting.

Create mystery

Do not open your first slide of a presentation with your solution. It's like giving someone an unwrapped gift for their birthday. You need an introductory slide or two (the wrapping paper) that builds some tension for the viewer. When you reveal your solution to the client, you want them to feel a sense of relief because you made them eager and want to see what you've made.

Focus on the big ideas and tell a story

Non-designers do not need to know the hyper-specific details, such as color codes, typeface names, or other small details related to your designs. Instead, they need to know the *why* behind your concepts. How does this solve the project challenges? How does the solution relate to their target audience(s)? How does the solution stack up against their competitors? And if you can deliver this information in a narrative that takes the viewer on a journey and creates an emotional connection—even better. Storytelling in business settings has been proven to enhance learning over the straightforward presentation of data. Stories are engaging, make complex ideas understandable and memorable, and work for all different types of learners (visual, auditory, and kinesthetic).[2] If you want to successfully pitch your designs to your client, a story will be the best way to convince them of your thinking: according to *Harvard Business*, "Research confirms that well-designed stories are the most effective vehicle for exerting influence."

Educate without pretension

Part of our role as designer is to educate our clients about the power of design. Have you ever had a teacher that made you feel dumb? Don't be that kind of teacher. Go into the process with empathy for someone learning something new. Use metaphors, examples, and layman's terms to demonstrate your thinking. Imagine your trusted non-designer (my mom for me) is the audience, and ask yourself if they would understand the presentation? Your clients are not training to be designers, so avoid information overload and keep it simple. Give them opportunities to ask questions, and answer them with kindness and respect.

Use mock-ups

At Unsold Studio, we were once presenting a brand identity to an eye doctor, showing the logo and icons on nice white backgrounds. It was hard to read the client's expression until we showed her how the branding could work on an eyeglasses cleaning cloth. Her reaction was immediate and clear, "Oh my god, I love it!" Many of our clients are not able to visualize the end result in the same way we are, so giving context through tools such as mock-ups is a useful aid for them. Alessandra Corbett from The Homegrown Studio (interview page 32) agrees: "Once they see it on a T-shirt mock-up, they were just psyched. Mock-ups can really drive it home for the client."

Include prices and resources for your solutions

As mentioned, many of your clients will be budget conscious. By sharing production costs and expenses along with your ideas, clients can make informed choices, and it demonstrates you're invested in their bottom line.

Be confident

The goal of design presentations is to get the client onboard with your ideas and buy in. If you come across as less than pleased about what you're sharing, the client will mirror that energy. Confidence, even if you have to fake it, will be more persuasive. As you're presenting, if you notice an error and it's small, do not draw attention to it—keep moving along. If the error is unmissable—acknowledge it, then keep moving along.

End intentionally

Many emerging designers abruptly end their presentations with an awkward silence, shrug of the shoulders, and a trailing voice that says "That's all I have." This type of ending sucks all the air from the room. You want to end confidently, but also cue in the client that you're done so they know it's their turn to do something. Including a slide at the end that says "Thank you for listening," or "Questions and comments" easily accomplishes this.

Accept feedback

The team from OuterEdit (interview page 107) say,

> *Be ready for constructive feedback. It's something that can only help you, especially when you're starting out. You want to know what you're good at, and where you can get better. Take in all the advice and the feedback, then select what you want to invest and commit your time to getting better at it. You don't have to be good at everything; choose where to put your energy.*

If you need to break up

There will come a time when you will want to quit on a client—you're frustrated and want out. However, my best advice is to not make any rash decisions. Breaking up can create conflict and burn bridges, and you never know where the client might reappear in your future. If you're close to the natural end of a project, my advice is to push through and go your separate ways after that. However, if you determine that terminating the project is in everyone's best interest, follow the cancellation clause as outlined in the terms and conditions of your proposal.

If you have broken up with the client, head back to Chapter 1, "If you need to find a freelance project." If you are sticking it out, head to Chapter 5, "When the project ends."

Interview

Nuevo Studio

Naoma Serna-Zahn is the founder and brand strategist at Nuevo Studio, an award-winning branding and graphic design firm located in Oklahoma City, Oklahoma. Originally from Mexico, her design story reflects characteristics often embodied by people willing to migrate to pursue their dreams: bravery, resiliency, and openness.

Throughout her career, Naoma has embraced change. Initially, she did not pursue design as a career path; her first degree is in French Literature and Culture. When she discovered her passion for graphic design, she returned to school for a second degree despite the doubts of her family and friends. Naoma has lived and worked

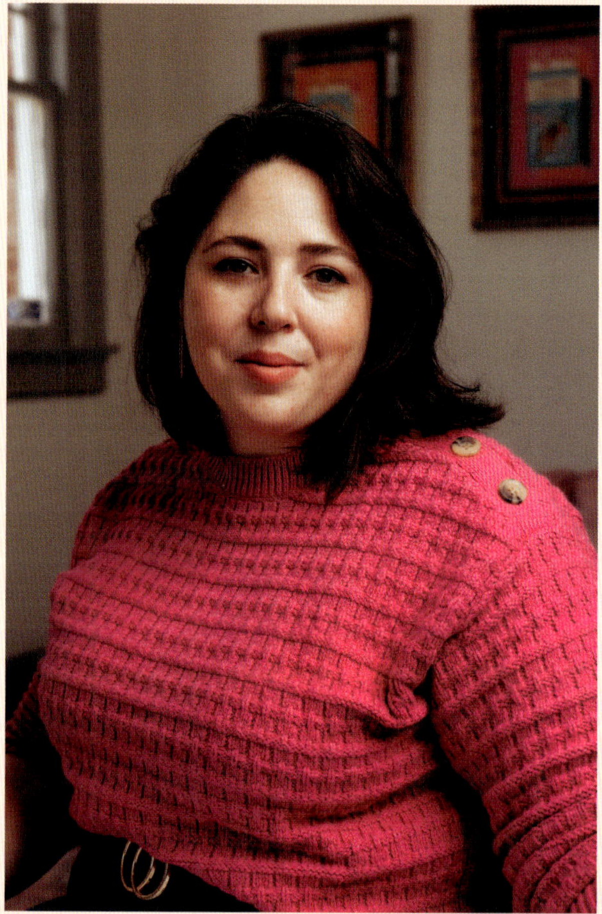

Figure 4.3 Naoma Serna-Zahn of Nuevo Studio. Image courtesy of Nuevo Studio.

in multiple countries, including France, Mexico, and the United States, adjusting to new cultures and communities. She began freelancing because it would enable her to have a "digital nomadic lifestyle" where she could travel and work, but she became rooted in an unexpected place: Oklahoma City. When her first design business ended, she tried again. Naoma proves pivoting, adapting, and starting over should not be feared along your design journey.

In the heartland

Naoma attended The School of Design at the University of Central Oklahoma in Edmond, Oklahoma, near Oklahoma City (aka OKC), because she had relatives living there, not because it was her first choice. A self-proclaimed traveler and foodie, Naoma was curious about the world. As a student, she thought, "I can't wait to get out of Oklahoma. I can't wait to go to New York, or Europe, or Portland, or Seattle, or somewhere else. I don't want to be here." She admits because she was so focused on her schoolwork, she missed that Oklahoma City had "been growing and getting cool." The city had added an NBA basketball team, local restaurants were getting nominated for James Beard Awards, and new buildings were being developed. Even with these changes happening locally, and Naoma landing a full-time design job in the city after graduation, she was not set on staying in OKC long term.

Newly engaged, Naoma and her partner decided they'd "hang out for a little bit in Oklahoma City." Her plan was to "get skin in the design game" and build a great portfolio so when they eventually moved away to a coastal city, she'd be competitive on the job market. However, the city grew on Naoma: "I realized I liked the energy here. People are so nice. Traffic is no more than twenty-minutes. We could afford to purchase our own home. Our quality of life here is great. I started to see myself as part of the community, and I wanted to build my design business and family there." Since this realization, her and her husband have made Oklahoma City their base, and they travel frequently to fulfill Naoma's wanderlust.

While she did not plan to settle in the middle of the United States, Naoma has built an award-winning firm by embracing the community there. Local clients such as the OKC Zoo, Asian District Cultural Association, William + Lauren, ADG Blatt, Elemental Coffee, Western Gateway School, and the National Women in Agriculture Association make up the majority of Nuevo Studio's portfolio. "I was just really frustrated with other local agencies that were essentially copying design work from bigger cities like Austin, Texas and looking like wannabes. There is definitely a culture here in Oklahoma that we could be cultivating and fostering and creating our own thing. And that's what I've been in pursuit of." These projects have garnered her studio recognition from *HOW*, *GDUSA*, the American Advertising Awards, and the Art Directors Club of Tulsa.

Outside of the studio, Naoma gives back to the creative community by serving as the President of the AMA (American Marketing Association) OKC, and previously as the President of the AIGA (American Institute of Graphic Arts; the professional association for design) Oklahoma and a former design educator at the School of Design at the University of Central Oklahoma. These roles have positioned her as a local leader, and allow her to easily meet nearby creatives, which has helped grow Nuevo Studio. "I know no one likes to hear how important networking is, but it's especially important in smaller towns and cities to know people in your industry; get to know everybody in your field. A lot of opportunities arise from other creatives."

In pursuit of freedom and feminism

Naoma credits two desires for beginning her full-time freelancing career; to have more autonomy in her work life and to better support women business owners. She wanted to take her laptop and work from overseas locations such as Thailand for months at a time. Unfortunately, her then full-time agency job was unwilling to make her request for remote work a reality. Continuing to work from her desk in the office, Naoma noticed that projects for women were not taken as seriously as others. "There would be logos created 'for women' and it was all calligraphy and watercolor. Like fine if you're a watercolor artist, but if you run a six- or seven-figure business, you need something more substantial." Seeing this need in the market, combined with her aspiration for more flexibility at work, Naoma decided it was time to start her own studio.

"I was a bit ignorant about what it takes to run a business. If I had known the grit it requires, I don't know if I would have done it that young without that much experience." While it all worked out for Naoma, she advises that it's important to learn about yourself as a designer before you invite clients into the mix. "When working with other designers, especially in agency environments, you learn that egos can hinder the design process. I learned how to communicate about design and wrangle with my own emotions in that setting before opening my own studio. Humility will make you a better business owner."

Naoma did not begin her first design business alone; she started with a partner. At the time, her and her collaborator were acquiring enough work that Naoma was able to quit her full-time agency job. Unfortunately, soon after she took that professional leap, her partner had a change of heart and decided to quit their business. "I was naïve enough to not even think about going back and getting another job. At that point, I said, 'Okay, I'm going to do this on my own.'"

Nuevo Studio was literally created over a weekend. When her partner left and dissolved their business, Naoma could not retain their name or the logo based on an agreement between them. She set out on a Friday to come up with a new name, logo, and brand so she could file a new LLC by Monday morning. Naoma asked her best friend to help manage some of the organizational tasks, so she could focus on the design side and keep the business afloat. Years later, that friend is now her Operations Manager overseeing their growing team and clientele, comprised of many women.

The big break

In the beginning, Naoma was scraping it together to make full-time freelancing work. "At one point, there was all sorts of random projects I took on because we needed the money; real estate flyers, social media graphics, cupcake liners." Nuevo Studio's first big and consistent client stemmed from an unexpected source: a Wes Anderson-themed art show.

Years before opening Nuevo Studio, Naoma displayed work in the whimsical gallery exhibition. At the opening event, she struck up a conversation with a fellow artist. They connected on social media, and the person saw examples of Naoma's design work on the platform. They then asked her to design posters for concerts and events at a local venue they managed called the Paramount Room. Naoma designed the posters for "very little money," but she credits that work for reconnecting her with an important person: an old college friend from her French degree program. The friend had become the righthand woman for a big film festival in Oklahoma City. They reached out to Naoma saying, "I like what you're making for the Paramount Room. Would you ever design some stuff for the deadCenter Film Festival?" *(A great reminder to be kind and stay in touch with your classmates!)*

Naoma said despite not knowing what the full extent of what designing for a citywide film festival would be, she said, "Yeah, I can totally do that," and learned on-the-go by "frantically googling at night." The deadCenter project came in Nuevo Studio's second year of business, when they were still relatively unknown, and put them on the map. "The film festival had previously worked with a big agency. Because I had taken this client from a bigger, flashier team, and I was a small one designing out of a co-working space, people were like, what's going on here?" She credits her competitive spirit for keeping her motivated and believing in running a boutique-sized studio: "It feels good giving other agencies a little bit of a tremble in the knees. I'm not competitive within my own team, but I like to remind our competitors we're still here. They'll have forty amazingly talented people, and our small team is competing for, and winning, the same design awards as them."

Seeing her deadCenter brand identity out in public was a turning point in Naoma's confidence. Nuevo Studio went on to design the film festival's look for three consecutive years, and that project led to other local clients seeking them out for work. She says she always smiles when she sees people wearing their T-shirt designs around town years later.

Challenges along the way

The journey to building Nuevo Studio has not always been easy. Around the same time the deadCenter project came in, Naoma also had her first big client issue: the person refused to pay the last 25 percent of the project fee. Before receiving this payment, Naoma had turned over the final design files to meet the client's tight deadline. In doing this, Naoma's kindness and flexibility meant she had lost her leverage to withhold the project deliverables until she was paid. "That was brutal. I had to get an attorney involved. And it happened over my birthday weekend."

Even though the outstanding bill was not a large sum of money, Naoma felt she had to pursue the issue on principle. "That was such a good learning experience. After that, I turned around and invested the money I finally received from the client back

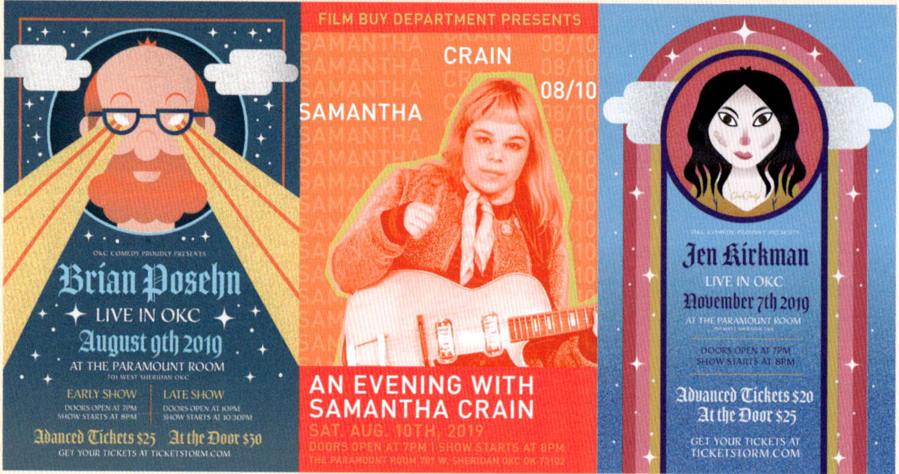

Figure 4.4 A sample of Nuevo Studio's work for the Paramount Room, which later led to other clients like deadCenter Film Festival. Image courtesy of Nuevo Studio.

into working with my lawyer to create a really good contract." With the new contract they developed, "it went from a one-page document to about twelve pages." Naoma says as she's encountered new challenges, she'll go back to her attorney to continuously update their contract.

For instance, now in Nuevo Studio's proposals they list client expectations to create clarity about the design process and timelines. "We underscore that our team is not solely responsible for meeting deadlines, because it is a collaborative process." Their document outlines that their team can make the project happen as planned, as long as the client makes themselves available for meetings and feedback.

Defining success

In the present, Naoma feels like she's finally acquiring the freedom she set out when she started her freelancing journey. In terms of creative freedom, her studio has worked hard to build a niche client roster that allows for challenging but rewarding work. "We've solidified the process of being able to create the kind of highly creative work I wanted to make in our community, and our clients trust us. I'm proud when folks come to me and say they feel seen, heard, and valued." A recent client, a custom suit maker in OKC, told Naoma that they "nailed it"; they loved the work for the branding platform and visual identity Nuevo Studio's team created. Those moments give Naoma "the high that we're doing good stuff to help people. That's worth more to me than a portfolio piece or an award."

Related to her desire to freelance to be free to globe trot, Naoma says:

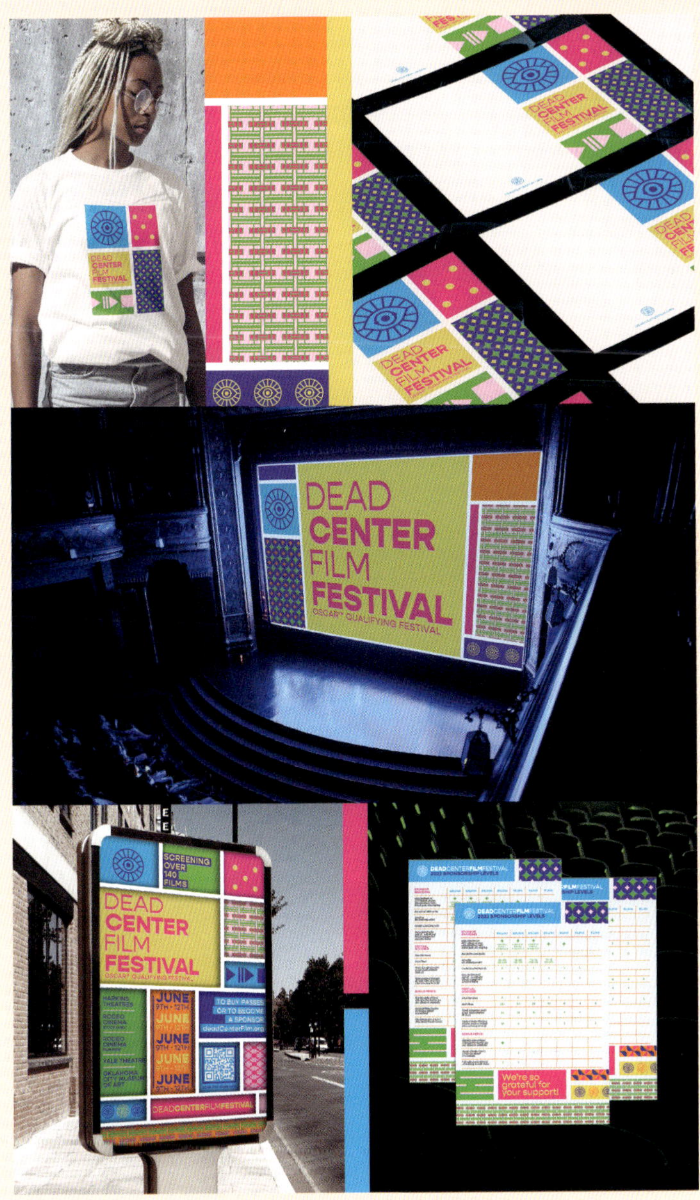

Figure 4.5 Nuevo Studio was inspired by the way stories have been told before film: through tapestry weavings. Pulling inspiration from patterns from Asia, Africa, South America, and Native America, they created a tapestry of the deadCenter Film Festival branding for 2022. Image courtesy of Nuevo Studio.

I did start this because I wanted to travel, work on a beach, wake up whenever I wanted to, but that has not really panned out. I have traveled, but it wasn't glamorous like I expected. For instance, I took my laptop to Thailand, but I'd have to get up early to work, and returning to answer emails at 9:00 p.m. after a full day of excursions. Now freedom means leaving work behind for a little while. I'm finally about to go on my first trip without my laptop.

However, during the COVID-19 pandemic she moved to Mexico for a year while everyone was working remotely. This allowed her to expand Nuevo Studio's reach to her hometown of San Miguel de Allende, Mexico. Naoma and her husband are now "toying with the idea of living part time in Mexico and part time in Oklahoma City." Perhaps Naoma is fulfilling all her initial dreams after all …

To learn more about Naoma and Nuevo Studio:

nuevo-studio.com
@nuevo.studio
@naoserna

5 When the project ends

The client might have exited the scene, but you still have a few things to do before you're done.

Document your work

Take it from a procrastinator; document your work right now—do not wait. Create images that are portfolio-worthy, write a project description, and put these files in a safe (backed-up) space on your computer. You will kick yourself later if these are not ready when you go to update your website, write a new proposal, or apply for an award. Even if you think this project is insignificant—do it; you might need a record of it someday. Once a potential client asked if Unsold Studio had experience designing wall graphics, and if so, to include examples in our proposal. We did, but we rarely documented this type of work in a high-quality way. Pulling together those work samples was a nightmare; tracking them down in unorganized folders took hours, then having to share poorly lit, low-resolution images with them was ... not great. The documentation did not reflect our skill level or professionalism accurately.

Also archive your process work and "failures" from the project. Do not throw them in your trash. You might decide to include them in a case study, recycle the solutions the client did not choose for a different project, or use it as content for social media.

As you do more freelancing work, it might be worth investing in a nice camera, higher quality mock-ups, or hiring a photographer to help you do this critical work. Potential clients use your portfolio to make a decision about hiring you, so do not let less-than documentation get in your way of landing jobs. If you think the finished project should be added to your public portfolio, return to "Curate your online presence," in Chapter 1. Consider if this addition should replace an existing one to best market your design services.

Follow up and gather data

A great habit to get into is following up with your clients for project data. For instance, six months after a project wraps, reach out and ask the client how your work has benefited their business. They might offer quantifiable data such as an increase in profits, or qualitative data, for instance, a great customer story. Either way, you can feature these successes online and in project proposals to help you garner more work.

By circling back to your clients, it is also a great excuse to reengage with them. Perhaps they have more work for you and have been meaning to reach out, or now that you're at the top of their mind, they will recommend your services to a friend. Continuing to check in with your clients like this is a great networking tool.

Keep a paper trail

You need to keep an archive of both your creative work and the business side of things for each project. Create a file naming and management system that allows you to easily search and find items you may need to reference in the future. If you need to clean-up file names that got messy, like finalfinalfinalfinal.psd, do this now.

When a project ends, do not delete all the design files related to the project. Store them somewhere safe (and backed up). The goal is to have return clients. At some point, they might return looking to make a 2.0 or 3.0 version of a project, and by having the original design files, the job will be much quicker. One time after accepting an update project like this, I realized I did not have the live file. What should have taken me five minutes ended up taking me over three hours because I had to search my unorganized laptop, then admit defeat and rebuild the file from scratch.

For your business records, keep items such as invoices, expenses, and receipts organized by year and client. If you're required to file taxes, this will streamline reporting your profits and losses. Additionally, archive proposals and addendums in the event legal issues arise in the future.

Brag a little

While it can feel gross to brag about yourself, folks need to know the great freelancing stuff you're doing for you to generate more opportunities (see "Shamelessly tell everyone," in Chapter 1, if you need a reminder). After you complete a project, it's a great time to:

- ***Feature project content on your website, on social media, an e-newsletter, and/or through other channels where you network.***

- ***Apply for design awards.*** Many professional design organizations have annual competitions, but there are also standalone awards. Usually these require an entry-fee, but they can help get you noticed and give credibility to your work in the eyes of a potential client if you win. Check out past winners to see if your project might be the right fit for what they typically select.
- ***Write a press release.*** Media outlets, particularly local ones, are often looking for stories. If you can provide them with a compelling narrative about your project, this could become free advertising for you. Think local news, magazines, blogs, and other outlets who tell stories like yours.
- ***Submit for a conference or speaking engagement.*** Use your project as a case study to educate an audience. The event does not have to be design-related; for example, designers John & Jane (interview, page 13) landed projects by speaking about branding at housing conferences.

Interview

Aaliyah Moore

Aaliyah Moore is an emerging designer and a beginner freelancer who represents many of you reading this book. She recently graduated in December 2022 with her Bachelor of Arts degree in Graphic Design with a minor in Art History from Oakland University in Rochester, Michigan. While a student, she was in the Honors College, made the Dean's List each semester, belonged to the Alpha Lambda Delta sorority, interned as a designer for the College of Arts and Sciences, oversaw students in the dorms as a Resident Advisor, and worked multiple jobs off-campus. Despite these accomplishments and experiences, she was nervous about her future in design.

To learn more about "the real world" in graphic design, she enrolled in my Professional Practices course, which this book is based on. In the class, she learned about multiple potential paths her career could take, such as working at a design firm or as a freelancer. Since graduating and entering the industry, her trajectory has included a mix of both; she's currently working as a graphic designer at Wee Lions Early Learning, while taking on a freelance project here and there. Aaliyah's goal is to run her own design business someday, but for now, she's continuing to learn from others and build her portfolio.

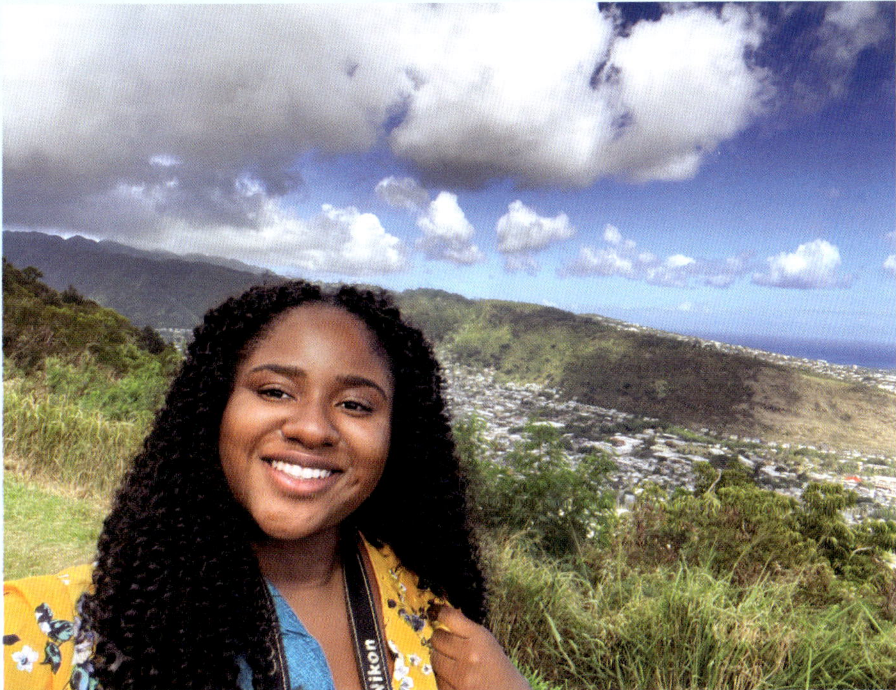

Figure 5.1 Aaliyah Moore. Image courtesy of Aaliyah Moore.

Aaliyah serves as an example that freelancing does not have to be an all-or-nothing approach. Her strategy to maintain a full-time job, while designing after-hours for her own clients is what I often recommend to newbies. If Aaliyah jumped right into running her own design business without much experience, she'd be learning how to manage client expectations, day-to-day tasks such as invoicing, and design work on top of ensuring she can make enough money to provide for herself. For now, her day job provides stability, while her occasional independent work allows her to flex her "freelancing muscles" without undue stress. When she's taken on projects outside of her day job, she's implemented contracts, pricing, and project management skills she learned in Professional Practices. When Aaliyah's ready to quit her day job and go full-time freelance, the transition will be smoother because she's built these good habits. I hope you'll be inspired by my former student, now friend, who's figuring it all out in live time like you.

It's normal to be intimidated

Aaliyah wants to run her own design studio in the future to create a legacy for herself and also to empower others. "I don't think there are many women who run their own design businesses, especially Black women." Aaliyah's instinct is correct: according to the *2019 AIGA Design Census*, only 3 percent of professional designers identify as Black.[1] Now divide that number by adding in statistics related to Black women, then divide again for Black women who own design businesses, and it's much less than the initial 3 percent. As a Black woman in design, Aaliyah is already a trailblazer, but when she does open her own shop, she'll further impact our industry.

Even though Aaliyah is not full-time freelance yet, she's begun her journey. "I found it super intimidating, and I still do a little bit." The design aspect did not scare her, but the business side was the most mysterious part. She did not know how to price her work, invoice a client, or write a contract. One of the big question marks for Aaliyah was how to find clients. "I didn't understand how designers found projects, or what potential clients might look for when hiring a designer. Once you gave me some ideas about this, I felt comfortable reaching out into my own network." Soon after, she acquired a project for a family friend who wanted help redesigning her website. That client then recommended her to another friend who had a small cosmetology business that needed a business card design. While Aaliyah describes these projects as "little things," they built the foundation of her client work portfolio.

Aaliyah advises, "If working with clients on your own is something you want to do, you have to be willing to learn about it and to ask questions." And that's exactly what Aaliyah did when she took my course. While naturally shy, she was not afraid to raise her hand during a lecture, or to continue the conversation with me after class. By showing her interest in the subject this way, she also garnered my attention. During that semester, my cousin emailed asking if I had any designers that I could recommend for Open Up, a nonprofit that teaches "mindfulness tools through movement practices and interactive arts while centering people living with disabilities" located in Pittsburgh, Pennsylvania. Aaliyah was the first person I suggested for the remote project designing social media and promotional templates, which she later landed. I felt comfortable passing along Aaliyah's name because her design

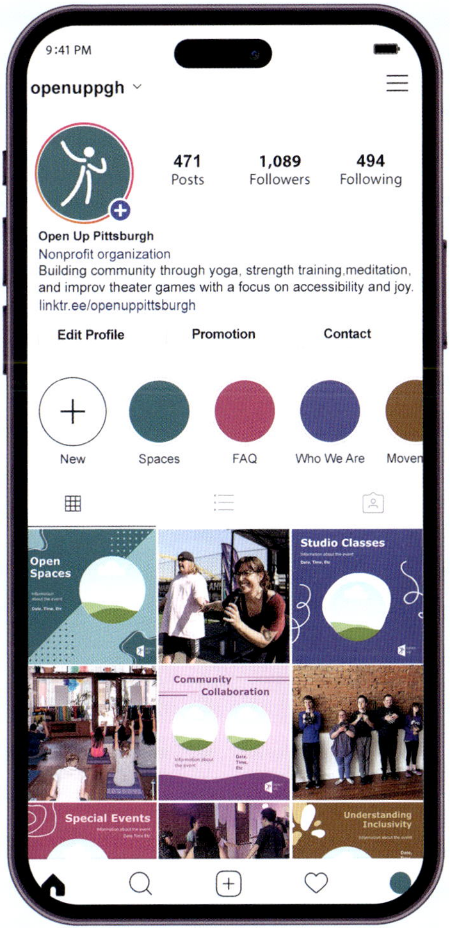

Figure 5.2 Aaliyah's Instagram profile mock-up for Open Up shows how her template designs will create consistency, without redundancy. Image courtesy of Aaliyah Moore.

work was strong, but more importantly, I knew she would provide a good experience for the client because she'd been so engaged in the Professional Practice course.

She says, "Don't let the fact that you're confused about how to do things scare you from actually starting. That was something that was holding me back initially. I felt like I couldn't start until I had learned *everything* about it." This need for perfection before beginning is common, especially for women. According to *Time* magazine's 2014 article "It's Not You, It's Science: How Perfectionism Holds Women Back" by

Jessica Bennett: "Women are more likely than men to be perfectionists, holding themselves back from answering a question, applying for a new job, asking for a raise, until they're absolutely 100% sure we can predict the outcome. (Women applied for a promotion only when they met 100% of the qualifications. Men applied when they met 50%.)"[2]

Organize yourself through the proposal

One of the best tools Aaliyah has implemented for her freelancing projects is a formal proposal for a prospective client. "Potential clients often have a lot of big ideas for what they want me to design for them, and the initial conversations can be scattered and overwhelming." To find clarity, Aaliyah uses a proposal template to organize all the information she gathers from those first conversations. "For a recent project, I wrote down every deliverable the person said. I didn't think at the end of the day she wanted or needed everything she mentioned, but I put it all in there in an organized list so she could see what I took out of our meeting and that I was listening closely to her." Once Aaliyah sent the proposal to the client, they had a conversation together to refine the project scope before agreeing to work together.

> **Initially, she wanted me to design fifteen different static social media posts, but once we reviewed the list in the proposal, we realized some of them were similar to one another. We decided to shorten the list and make templates based on categories instead. This helped better meet her budget because it would take me less time to produce the templates. It was also a better investment for her because templates would allow her to create endless posts, rather than the initial scope of fifteen fixed posts.**

Aaliyah's proposal document also contains a suggested timeline for the project, which took her a few times to refine. "At first, I didn't necessarily make the schedule in a way that made sense." Her first drafts of timelines were too rushed. "I forgot that my client is a busy business owner and would need more time than I initially planned for to provide me feedback. I learned to ask my potential clients about their average response time for emails and built the project schedule to account for their working style, not just mine."

Don't be afraid to guide the client

While a student, Aaliyah landed a freelance project for the Native American Advisory Committee (NAAC) at our university. (I recommended her for this as well—a good reminder to network with your professors!) "It was the first time I was working with someone who was not familiar with design. For instance, the client gave me

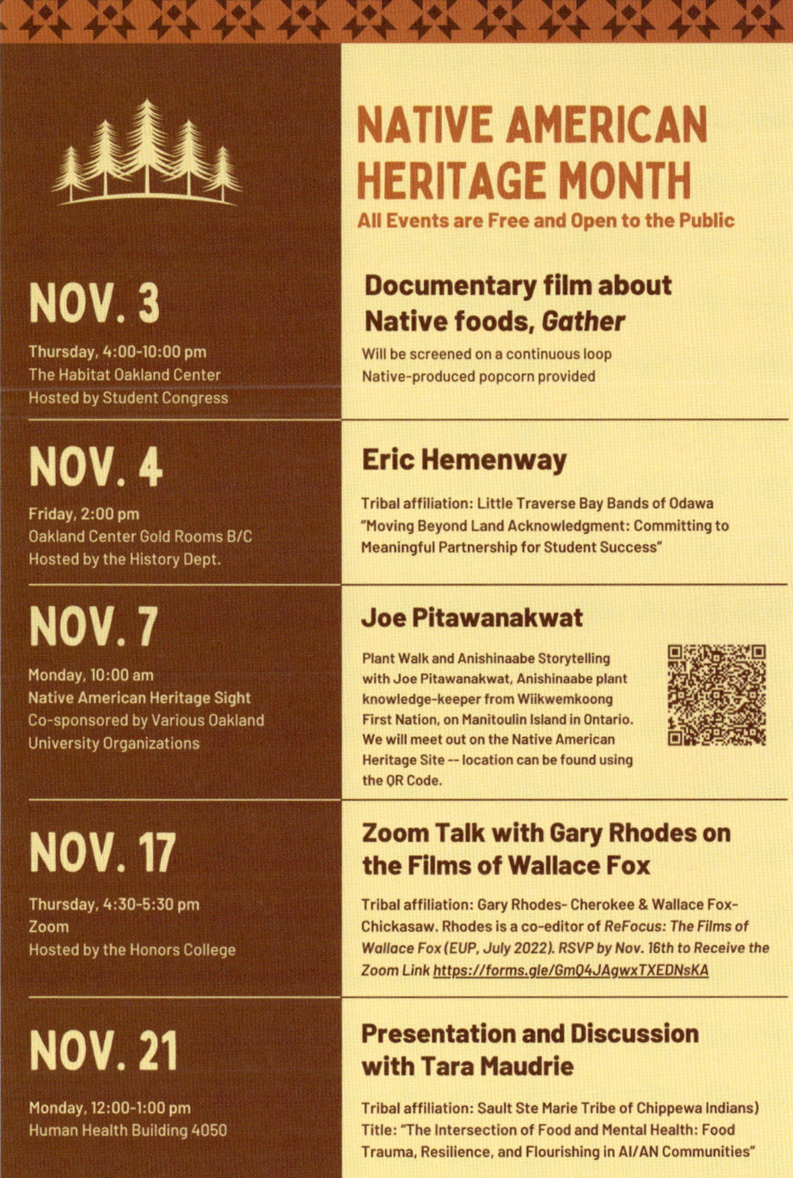

Figure 5.3 Aaliyah's final flyer design for Native American Heritage Month for her client, Oakland University's Native American Advisory Committee (NAAC). Image courtesy of Aaliyah Moore.

way too much text to fit on the size flyer they wanted." Instead of trying to force all the text on the deliverable to please the client, but result in an ineffective design, Aaliyah suggested a few changes. For example, she encouraged them to shorten the event descriptions, and instead of including a long link to guide folks to the event location, she advocated for a QR code to scan instead. She was nervous about stepping on the client's toes, but she knew these changes would better meet the project goals. Aaliyah says she relied on skills she acquired working at her non-design jobs to communicate suggested changes to the client:

> **When I worked as a customer service representative at a retail store and as a server at a restaurant, I learned a lot about patience and communicating with others. I tapped into these skills to approach my client about why these edits were important to make. It's interesting that I thought these types of job would not directly help my design career, but they definitely have.**

Luckily, the client was positive and receptive to her suggestions, especially when Aaliyah visually demonstrated the differences between the design with the initial content the client provided, and the design with the suggested shorter content.

The project also called for Aaliyah to create imagery for the flyer. "Initially, the client wanted to have an illustration of Native American people, but it was difficult to be inclusive and represent the variety of people within the community on a small card that already had a lot of text. Instead, we worked together to decide on a symbol of their community, which ended up being a tree." Aaliyah's advocacy for another direction for the image resulted in another positive outcome for the project; the NAAC team was so pleased with her work that they continue to use her icon of the tree on their promotional materials.

Take it slow and steady

While her full-time job designing children's educational books takes up most of her attention right now, she's continuing to pick up client work. Aaliyah says she still struggles with pricing her work and is refining her proposal templates and contract as she goes, but she's making progress toward her long-term vision for her design career. She has her first return client, which speaks to the great service she provided them if they're coming back to her for more design work. Keep an eye out for Aaliyah; she's making freelancing moves right alongside you.

To learn more about Aaliyah Moore:

aaliyahmoore.myportfolio.com
@liyah0101

Celebrate yourself

When we're busy, we forget to look back and see how far we've come. Take a second and appreciate that you did it—you completed a successful freelance design project! You might feel like there's room for improvement, but there always is. I'm proud of you, and I hope you're proud of you too.

Once you've celebrated, head right on back to Chapter 1, "If you need to find a freelance project." The work isn't done—you have to keep pursuing your freelancing dreams and empowering others with your design skills, especially those close to home.

Resources

Keywords

addendum An add-on to an agreement that outlines updates and changes.

case study A detailed description of a portfolio project that shows the different phases of your design process and demonstrates your thinking and problem-solving.

cold call Reaching out to someone you have not interacted with before to generate project leads.

DBA In the United States, a legal term that stands for "Doing Business As."

deposit An upfront payment of 25–50 percent of the total project estimate that commits the client and the designer to the project.

design brief A one- or two-page document that summarizes key elements of a project to keep you and the client on task; it functions like your project "assignment sheet."

EIN In the United States, a legal term that stands for "Employer Identification Number," which certain business structures require to file taxes and open various accounts.

force majeure clause A French term that translates as "superior force,"[1] which absolves liability in the event of reasons beyond your control.

LLC In the United States, a legal term that stands for "Limited Liability Company," a business structure that protects the business owner from personal liability in most instances, in case of bankruptcy or lawsuits.

market rate The standard price for services; not discounted.

overhead Expenses that you generally require to freelance and are not tied directly to a specific project or client.

pro bono Volunteer-based work, generally for projects that benefit the public good.

project scope The requirements and limits of the job such as deliverables, timeline, and budget.

RFP A term that stands for "Request for Proposal."

scope creep Increasing the project scope beyond the agreement between the client and the designer.

spec work When a designer provides creative work to a client prior to receiving compensation.

sub-contracting When an individual or company hires someone outside of their team to fulfill part or all of their duties on a specific project.

Business tools I use

Accounting/Invoicing/Time Tracking: Freshbooks (Toggl is a free time tracker for individuals)

Email (plus Calendar and File Back-up): Google Workspace

Project management: Trello

Website Builder: Squarespace

Further reading

Airey, David. *Work for Money, Design for Love: Answers to the Most Frequently Asked Questions About Starting and Running a Successful Design Business (Voices That Matter)*, 1st edn. San Francisco, CA: New Riders, 2012.

Barton, Gem. *Don't Get a Job … Make a Job: Inventive Career Models for Next-gen Creatives*, new edn. London: Laurence King Publishing, 2023.

Branagan, Alison. *The Essential Guide to Business for Artists and Designers*, 2nd edn. London: Bloomsbury Visual Arts, 2020.

Feldman, David. *Small By Design: The Entrepreneur's Guide for Growing Big While Staying Small*. New York: Morgan James Publishing, 2022.

Graphic Artists Guild, The. *Graphic Artists Guild Handbook, Pricing & Ethical Guidelines*, 16th edn. Cambridge, MA: The MIT Press, 2021.

Griffo, Ilana. *Mind Your Business: A Workbook to Grow Your Creative Passion into a Full-time Gig*. Bend, OR: Paige Tate & Co, 2019.

Janda, Michael. *The Psychology of Graphic Design Pricing: Price Creative Work with Confidence. Win More Bids. Make More Money*. Self-published, 2019.

Notes

Prelims

1 Gilson, Stuart, Kristin Mugford, and Annelena Lobb, "Bankruptcy in the City of Detroit," Harvard Business School Case 215-070, April 2015 (revised April 2022).
2 "Graphic Designers: Occupational Outlook Handbook: U.S. Bureau of Labor Statistics," September 6, 2023. Available online: https://www.bls.gov/ooh/arts-and-design/graphic-designers.htm#tab-3 (accessed August 18, 2024).
3 "Freelancing in America: 2019," Slide show, PPT, September 23, 2019. Available online: https://www.slideshare.net/upwork/freelancing-in-america-2019 (accessed August 18, 2024).

Chapter 1

1 US Small Business Administration, "Register Your Business," n.d. Available online: https://www.sba.gov/business-guide/launch-your-business/register-your-business (accessed August 18, 2024).
2 US Small Business Administration, "Choose a Business Structure," n.d. Available online: https://www.sba.gov/business-guide/launch-your-business/choose-business-structure (accessed August 18, 2024).
3 CreativeMornings, "CreativeMornings | Breakfast Lecture Series for the Creative Community," n.d. Available online: https://creativemornings.com/ (accessed August 18, 2024).
4 Ibid.
5 Benedict Sheppard, Hugo Sarrazin, Garen Kouyoumjian, and Fabricio Dore, "The Business Value of Design," McKinsey & Company, October 25, 2018. Available online: https://www.mckinsey.com/capabilities/mckinsey-design/our-insights/the-business-value-of-design (accessed August 18, 2024).

Chapter 3

1 *Merriam-Webster's Collegiate Dictionary*, 11th edn (Springfield, MA: Merriam-Webster, 2004).

Chapter 4

1 Thomas M. Sullivan, "Small Business Weekly Forecast," US Chamber of Commerce, December 29, 2023. Available online: https://www.uschamber.com/small-business/small-business-weekly-forecast (accessed August 18, 2024).
2 Vanessa Boris, "What Makes Storytelling so Effective for Learning?" Harvard Business Publishing, December 20, 2017. Available online: https://www.harvardbusiness.org/what-makes-storytelling-so-effective-for-learning/ (accessed August 18, 2024).

Chapter 5

1 Meg Miller, "The Design Collective Taking on Structural Racism in the Industry," Eye on Design, July 2, 2020. Available online: https://eyeondesign.aiga.org/the-design-collective-taking-on-structural-racism-in-the-industry/ (accessed August 18, 2024).
2 Jessica Bennett, "It's Not You, It's Science: How Perfectionism Holds Women Back," TIME, April 22, 2014. Available online: https://time.com/70558/its-not-you-its-science-how-perfectionism-holds-women-back/ (accessed August 18, 2024).

Resources

1 *Merriam-Webster's Collegiate Dictionary*, 11th edn (Springfield, MA: Merriam-Webster, 2004).

Index